KEEPING THE DOORS OPEN

KEEPING THE DOORS OPEN

PETER LORD

Unless otherwise identified, Scripture quotations are taken from the *New American Standard Bible,* copyright © 1960, 1962, 1963, 1968, 1971, 1972, 1973, 1975, 1977 by the Lockman Foundation. Used by permission.

Scripture quotations identified KJV are from the King James Version of the Bible

Library of Congress Cataloging-in-Publication Data

Lord, Peter, 1929–
Keeping the doors open / Peter Lord.
p. cm.
ISBN 0-8007-9198-3
1. Faith development. 2. Parenting—Religious aspects—Christianity. 3. Children—Religious Life. 4. Lord, Peter, 1929–
I. Title.
BV4637.L64 1992
248.8'45—dc20 91-44900

A Chosen Book

Published by Chosen Books Publishing
a division of Baker Book House Company
P.O. Box 6287, Grand Rapids, Michigan 49516-6287

ISBN: 0-8007-9198-3

Second printing, August 1992

Printed in the United States of America

To our children
John; Richard and Debbie; Susan and Eli
Jimmy and Melinda; Ruth and Keith
for their love and patience
beyond the call of duty

Many thanks to
Christine W. Greenwald
for her editorial expertise and
finishing touches on this manuscript

Contents

Introduction

Some time ago our son Richard, a husband, father of five boys and pastor, said to me, "Rearing children is not a science, it's an art. In a science, you do the same things over and over again and come up with the same results. But in art each piece is an original."

Richard is right: Each child *is* an original, a unique individual, unlike any person in the whole world. And in the spiritual realm, children who come to God grow in the Christian faith at their own paces, in God's time. Yet how difficult it is for us as Christian parents when our children struggle with temptations and rebellions, when they reject God. We worry and wonder: Will they ever come back?

It is then we must, as the great missionary and devotional writer Oswald Chambers put it in his classic book, *My Utmost for His Highest,* "Let God be as original with other people as He is with you." If we have the promise of God for our children, we can know with certainty that He will fulfill it in His own time, in His own way.

In Section 1 of this book I discuss the process by which parents and their children can move from fear and rebellion to faith and redemption, from sorrow to joy. In Section 2 I share principles my wife, Johnnie, and I have learned as we have tried to follow God's patterns for parenting, allowing the Holy Spirit to work in each of our children in His own original way, using us as He wills in the process.

This book is a testimony to the grace of God. We have made our share of mistakes in rearing our children, but God is good, and is dealing with each of them as only the Father of all fathers, the inventor of fatherhood, knows best to do.

My prayer for this book is:

Dear God our Father, God of mercy,

Create in the hearts of all the readers of this book revelation about Your grace, mercy and power: Your grace that forgives and offers second, third and many more opportunities; Your mercy that triumphs over judgment; and Your power to turn any life and situation around. We thank You for Your ability to do exceedingly abundantly above all that we can ask or even think.

Praise Your holy name! Amen.

Peter Lord
Titusville, Florida
Fall 1991

KEEPING THE DOORS OPEN

Section 1

The Process

1

Building Blocks: The Basis for This Book

At five o'clock one spring morning in 1972 the telephone rang in our Titusville, Florida, home, waking my wife, Johnnie, and me from a sound sleep.

"We have your son here," said a deep voice on the other end of the line. Identifying himself as the desk sergeant at the Orlando jail about forty miles away, he explained that our twenty-year-old son, Richard, had been arrested and charged with possession of narcotics.

I do not need to tell you that this is a most unpleasant way to awaken early in the morning. Neither do I need to explain why I have no trouble remembering how it felt to see my firstborn behind bars later that day. The scene is indelibly fixed in my mind some twenty years after it happened.

There was Richard in dirty dungarees and T-shirt, barefoot, with his long, uncombed hair falling over his shoulders. He was subdued and quiet. I do not know what he expected us to do, but we had told him over and over that if his drug use led him to jail we would not bail him out.

Difficult as it was, and despite the sadness and hurt we felt as we stood in the jail corridor talking with him, we stuck by our word. When we headed for home we left, instead of bail money, strong assurances of our love and our willingness to help him when he was ready to change.

Underneath all of the other emotions we experienced as we drove home that day was a quiet confidence that God was in control. We were learning that the most important tools for relating to our Lord Jesus—tools we had each learned through our own personal crises of faith, tools we will discuss later in this chapter—applied also to this crucial arena of training our children to be responsible and (we prayed) God-fearing Christian adults.

But, like millions of Christian parents before us, we faced a grim reality: Despite our prayers and concerted efforts to raise our children according to our understanding of biblical principles, our eldest son was not behaving in either a responsible or a Christlike manner. He had, at least for a time, left God. And, as you will discover in the pages of this book, over the years we have experienced varying degrees of anxiety and crisis over our four other children as well.

But praise God! This book is about His graciousness, both in teaching and molding our children, and in teaching and molding Johnnie and me through our parenting ups and downs. I have made many mistakes in rearing our children, and in being a husband (which is a vital part of rearing children). Yet our Father and Lord has helped us and is restoring the years the locusts have eaten (see Joel 2:25). He has done exceedingly above all I asked for or imagined!

What to Look For

Most likely you have purchased this book because you, too, are a parent in crisis—a parent who is watching, brokenhearted, frustrated and maybe very angry, as your child or children seemingly turn their backs on the values you have tried to instill in them. They, too, have left God. It is my desire that you will find in this book two kinds of help.

First, I hope you will find workable encouragement for your present crisis. Second, I hope you will find guidelines for preventing or at least alleviating some future crises by improving your parenting know-how and sensitivity. Parenting is one of the few professions in life for which most of us have little or no training. We're bound to make mistakes, but each lesson we learn makes us better equipped to handle the next challenge.

There are also two traps any writer on this subject must take care to avoid, and each reader must be on the alert for them, as well.

The first trap is this: looking for a "sure-fire" formula for rearing children.

In my own experience in rearing both our natural children and the spiritual children over whom the Father has given me watchcare duties, I have found that child-rearing at its best is not done by factory and formula; it is done by research and development. Let me explain.

Most modern factories use the assembly line method. If the workers perform the same functions in the same way under the same conditions they will end up with the same products. So the Pontiac 6000s that roll off the line might vary in color and a few accessories, but they are basically alike.

Using a formula is appealing. It looks easy and foolproof. In fact, many books, seminars and sermons on child-rearing offer formulas: "Fifteen Steps to Rearing Successful (or Godly or Christian) Children."

These formulas usually come from two basic types of people. The worse of the two is the writer or speaker who has never reared a child successfully but has devised a theory by threading together various Bible verses.

Why is this so bad? Because by using half a verse here and a third of a verse there he or she can prove almost anything from Scripture. And most of what he or she "proves" is not consistent with God's Word. The Scriptures offer plain and simple truths, guidelines and principles. They do not need elaborate interpretation. They were written for the common man and woman, and can be understood easily and simply.

The other formula-oriented person is the one whose children turned out to be godly. These sincere and earnest Christians sought God's wisdom on their knees in rearing their children for His honor and glory. Their mistake is in believing that what worked for them will work for everyone else.

And why doesn't it? Because the formula assumes that all children are the same at the beginning. If parents begin with the same "raw materials" each time and apply certain "tried and true" methods, they will end up with the same results.

But no child is the same. One of the most amazing things about children is how they can come from the same parents and be so completely different in almost every way! They are living beings, life forms. Written into each one at the moment of conception are inherent qualities that, through their parents' cooperation with God or lack of it, can be developed or squashed.

When you build something you have the privilege of designing what you want and then producing it. When you grow a life form, the predetermined design is already there and you can only cooperate with it. Each child is a completely individual package of potential. Each will end up not as a clone, but as a special expression of God's creative power.

This is where research and development comes in. You see, in industry the research and development department is where prototypes are created. Each project is new, different. Special attention is given to every detail because the end result will be like no other.

Thus, as parents prepare to raise each child they must approach each one as a separate project—as an exercise in research and development, in growing and shaping, not building. To do this they need the Holy Spirit's help to find out how best to cooperate with the life of each child in maximizing the unique combination of qualities God has given him or her.

So while I won't be sharing a formula for successful child-rearing I will be sharing the principles that Johnnie and I have learned from our Lord and Father as we have muddled our way into and through a variety of child-rearing crises, both small and large. But principles have a thousand applications—applications that will differ in every circumstance and must be interpreted to us individually by the Holy Spirit.

So leave behind the first trap of looking for a formula. Instead seek the hope and encouragement that God in His grace and mercy will draw both you and your children closer to Himself.

The second trap is this: falling into guilt trips.

The last thing I want to do is act as the devil's travel agent and send parents with erring children on another guilt trip. Many books, articles, sermons and conferences on parenting convinced me more of my failures than of the power of God to take my attempts at parenting and use them to teach our whole family more about Him.

Remember, we have all made mistakes. But if we have repented and asked God to forgive us and help us to listen for His guidance as we parent, we need feel no more guilt. If we do, we can know it is motivated by the devil, who delights in halting our forward progress by accusing us continually of past failures.

The devil even uses Scripture to make parents feel guilty. Think of that verse so often quoted by writers and teachers: "Train up a child in the way he should go, even when he is old he will not depart from it" (Proverbs 22:6). How easily the devil can twist this wonderful text to accuse and wound already hurting mothers and fathers!

"If you had done right your children would have turned out right," Satan whispers. "You failed, and that is why they have gone astray."

There is enough logic in Satan's accusation to drive even fairly strong Christians to heavy guilt. But a fundamental mistake so many of us make as parents is to believe the enormous lie implicit in Satan's twisted logic.

What lie? you ask. Just this: Children become godly because their parents do the "correct" things in raising them.

This is simply not true. *Only God can make anyone godly*, and we will explore that concept further in the following chapters. But to believe that our parental actions can produce godly children reduces genuine Christianity to a formula, and God will not be reduced to a formula. He is sovereign, bigger and stronger and wiser than we can ever imagine, and to think that the building of godly children rests on our puny efforts alone is ridiculous.

Building Blocks

Keeping the Doors Open is founded on two vital premises, or building blocks. Unless we understand and incorporate them into our lives, the rest of the book will be meaningless. Please read the remainder of this chapter carefully and prayerfully, asking God to help you make these building blocks the foundation for your whole life with Him, including your vitally important mission as a Christian parent.

Building Block 1: *Christian parents need to relate intimately to God the Father, Son and Holy Spirit—to come to know Him—through study of and meditation on Scripture and two-way communication.*

How basic, you say! Yes, it is, but far too many Christian parents rely on a Sunday morning spoon-feeding session and nightly table grace to nurture the relationship begun with God when they accepted Jesus as Savior. Then they flail and flounder through parenting situations wondering why God doesn't give them the wisdom and assistance they need.

But the emphasis in Scripture is on knowing God. The word *know* in the Bible is used to mean much more than does our common usage, which implies "to know about." *To know* in the Bible indicates an intimate personal experience; in fact, it is the word used throughout the Scripture to describe sexual intercourse. To achieve intimacy with God, a personal and deep relationship with Him, is by far the highest pursuit in life.

The apostle Paul, from his jail cell in Rome, wrote to the Philippian church that all the things he had done and experienced were dung—manure!—compared to the value of *knowing* Christ Jesus as his Lord. And this was the man who started at least thirteen churches and was the primary apostle and witness for Jesus Christ in his day.

How Can We Know God?

We get to know God the same as we get to know most people: in private. By being alone together people are freer to share at the deepest levels and thus to know each other's hearts.

The best and easiest way I have found to know God is to establish a regular quiet time and place, away from the distractions of life, where I can give full attention to my heavenly Father and the Lord Jesus Christ. It is possible, of course, to hear God speak anytime and anywhere He wishes and chooses to speak. But by learning to hear Him speak in private we will more easily recognize His voice at other times, including those of chaos and stress.

Besides, one of the greatest honors we can give to anyone is our time and undivided attention. I've learned that when I make and keep appointments with God He is pleased to meet with me.

Sitting at Jesus' feet and listening to His Word is the one essential no Christian—and no Christian parent—can disregard. Let me say it again—this is one of two building blocks on which this whole book rests.

Jesus emphasized the importance of this building block in this story:

> Now as they were traveling along, He entered a certain village; and a woman named Martha welcomed Him into her home. And she had a sister called Mary, who moreover was listening to the Lord's word, seated at His feet. But Martha was distracted with all her preparations; and she came up to Him, and said, "Lord, do You not care that my sister has left me to do all the serving alone? Then tell her to help me." But the Lord answered and said to her, "Martha, Martha, you are worried and bothered about so many things; but only a few things are necessary, really only one, for Mary has chosen the good part, which shall not be taken away from her."
>
> Luke 10:38–42

In their very helpful book *Discover Your God-Given Gifts* (based on Romans 12:6–8), authors Don and Katie Fortune point out that this passage shows Martha exercising her inborn gift of serving, and that Jesus no doubt complimented her on many occasions for the fine hospitality and quiet refuge she offered Him. But in this instance He wants her—and us—to see that our *service* to God is empty unless we truly *know* Him.

My quiet time has proven to be the best, most enjoyable and most profitable time of my life. Here I have found faith, encouragement, motivation and instruction for my whole life—including my tasks as a Christian parent. I compare my quiet time with my most intimate moments with my wife. Why? Because these are the closest times I have with the persons I love the most.

Developing a Profitable Quiet Time

There are many ways to spend quality time alone with God, and eventually most people develop their own styles, times and places. Having regular quiet times and keeping them private are important aspects, but they may vary occasionally as the circumstances of your life change. Don't "get the guilts" about this. Simply do your best to reestablish regularity and privacy again as soon as possible.

Many people include thanksgiving, praise and worship in their quiet times. Some use this time to read Christian literature. Whatever else you choose to include, two components are crucial: meditation on Scripture and prayer.

Meditating on Scripture. First of all, recognize that the Author of all Scripture, the Holy Spirit, lives in you. He knows His own Word, and He knows you and your situation. So go to your private place with a Bible, a pen and a notebook to record your impressions and your prayers. Pick a Bible book and plan to work through it. I suggest starting in the New Testament, preferably with one of the Gospels.

Then meditate on the Scripture you've chosen by reading slowly, always listening for the voice of the Author, who came to guide us into all truth. It is not the amount of Scripture we read that is beneficial, but the amount of truth that winds up in our hearts. A person can own a grocery store, work in it several times a day and still starve to death. Only by consuming food does he gain the nourishment he needs. The same is true in our spiritual lives.

How does Scripture meditation differ from Bible study? A person studies with his or her left brain, and meditates with his or her right brain. It works like this.

The left brain stores all the information that comes into each of our lives. With this information we reason, figure and conclude. But we can reason only on the basis of the facts stored in this "computer." If we have only partial facts or incorrect information our conclusions are confined by those limits.

The right brain, on the other hand, has fascinating capacities like imagination—the ability to see what is not present in time or space. It receives new information and can pick up messages from the spirit worlds, both God's and the devil's.

Thus, when we study the Bible we use our accumulated information (true or false) to form conclusions. Remember, we act according to what we believe to be true whether it is true or not. That is why some Christians who lived during the Civil War were able to claim that God condoned human slavery. Their study of the Bible and the information they had accumulated from the outside world through the left brain combined to present what they thought was a correct conclusion.

To meditate on the Bible we open our minds to the Holy Spirit. We allow Him to call up information from the left side of our brains and to communicate through the right side as well. He may bring to mind a certain fact or point out false information and then renew our minds with right and true information. He may inspire our imaginations to picture different Bible characters in recorded incidents, and help us apply that understanding to our own situations. And He may give us His intuition to discern the correctness of motives and actions, our own and those of the people around us.

Meditation is a wonderful way to read the Scriptures, to let the Author, who knows you and knows His own Word, put together just the nourishment you need. I wish someone had taught me how to meditate early in my Christian life. Sitting at Jesus' feet, listening to His Word and writing down my impressions has been immensely helpful and practical as I have worked through difficult child-rearing problems.

Profiting by Prayer. The second crucial component of the quiet time is prayer. That's how most Christians through the ages have fellowshiped with God; the majority of them never had Bibles, or access to Bibles, and couldn't have read them anyway. Yet they were able to know, learn to trust and maintain fellowship with God through prayer.

How did they do it? After all, many new Christians start out enthusiastically in prayer, only to stop praying, eventually, in any meaningful way. That's perfectly natural because few of us practice prayer as a means of fellowship with God. Instead it is simply a one-way conversation, often filled with "gimmes." Understandably, most intelligent people become bored.

But when prayer is a conversation between you and the God who loves you it is wonderful experience.

How good God is to allow the Holy Spirit to live in us and guide us in our praying, since so often we do not know how to pray (Romans 8:26–27)! As we fellowship with Him during our quiet times we are free to ask Him anything on our hearts, and He is free to speak to us about the burdens He knows we carry.

One day as I was asking God how to pray for one of our daughters, He said, *Ask Me to protect her.* That is exactly what I did. Imagine how I felt when I heard, later that afternoon, that she had been in an accident. Her car was fully demolished, but she came out of the smashup completely whole!

Prayer time should be conversation time, when I can pray or act with God's wisdom and power. I have found that when I do as He says, it frees Him to do as He wills and wants to do.

Meditation on Scripture, which trains us to hear His voice, is critical to this kind of praying. Without the ability to hear His voice, we will pray only from our own points of view.

Building Block 2: *Christian parents need to cooperate with God by carrying out whatever actions He impresses on us as we relate to Him.*

This entire book is built around the absolute necessity for hearing the God who guides us into all truth and gives all wisdom and support with supernatural power. We need to spend time with the One who cares for us and our children more than we can ever imagine, who knows our heartaches and our children's problems, and who can offer real and permanent answers.

William Hay M. H. Aitken wrote,

> Whatever happens let us not be too busy to sit at Jesus' feet. We shall not . . . lose time by enjoying this; . . . we shall redeem the time . . . and we shall gain in blessedness and enjoyment of our work, and gain in the quality of our work; and, above all, we shall gain in that we shall give Him pleasure where otherwise we might only grieve Him. And this is indeed the crown of all our endeavors. *He who pleases Him does not live in vain.*

God has often impressed upon me, as I have shared my concerns about my children with Him, that I was to pray a certain way, make a telephone call, write a letter or arrange for some one-on-one time with one of my children. When I obey those impressions and act on the directions He offers, another piece of the puzzle or problem concerning that child falls into place, whether I know it at the time or not. But if I fail to obey that impression, I hinder His Spirit from continuing to work in my child's life.

What a blessing to be able to take each of our children's problems or needs, each distressing incident or behavior, each call for concern, into our quiet times with the Lord! As we meditate on Scripture and talk with Him, He gives us wisdom, unconditional love for our children, creativity and ideas for handling each situation.

Now obviously this building block stands in direct opposition to the way so many of us deal with our children: flying blind as we *react*—both emotionally and physically—to our children's attitudes and behavior. How often, instead of taking a concern to my quiet time and waiting for my Father's directions, I have answered with anger or harshness or lack of compassion, and made a parent-child situation much worse!

Remember: Cooperation with God takes practice. It becomes part of the spiritual nature only after we learn to know His voice and relate to Him intimately. But the rewards are worth the effort, for we will begin to see Him work. And as we "cast our cares on Him," allowing *Him* to be responsible for developing godliness in our children, the burdens of parenting will become lighter and the road ahead brighter.

In the next chapter, by sharing some of the events that led Richard, Johnnie and me to that sad encounter in the Orlando jail, we will deal more specifically with the way to hear God's word for a particular problem with a particular child.

2

The Word of Faith

Principle: Faith stands on who God is and what He says. Before you can believe a promise for your child you must get a promise from God. Faith comes by hearing a word from God.

Scripture: Isaiah 55:8-11; Romans 10:17

That Saturday morning in the spring of 1971 started as so many others had, with our family at different stages of wakefulness. Saturday at the Lord house was a day for sleeping in, family togetherness and catching up on household jobs.

Susan, our eighteen-year-old daughter, was eating breakfast. My wife, Johnnie, and Ruth Ann, our ten-year-old, were getting dressed. Richard, nineteen, and one-year-old John, our baby, were still in bed. (Jimmy had not yet joined our family.)

As I prepared to do some chores, a knock sounded at the door. I answered and found Bill, our church's minister of youth and music, standing there.

"I need to talk to you and Johnnie," he said quietly.

I called Johnnie, and we invited Bill into the living room and sat down, a bit puzzled by his serious expression.

"Has Richard talked to you?" Bill asked.

"No," we replied. "What about?"

Instead of answering, Bill asked, "Is Richard around? I'd really like him to be here while we talk."

It took a few minutes to get Richard out of bed, but finally all four of us were seated in the living room together.

Then Bill said, "I gave Richard a week to tell you something, and told him if he had not done so by today I would come and speak to you."

Bill was about to drop a bomb on us, a bomb that would begin a new phase in our parenting experience and change our lives forever, especially our relationships with God and each member of our family.

He said simply, "Richard is on drugs."

Richard, our eldest child, had been elected the most popular boy in the graduating class his senior year in high school. He had always been a nice, easygoing fellow. We were sorry he had dropped out from his freshman year in junior college, but he seemed happy working at a local men's clothing store.

But Richard on drugs? *Our* Richard on drugs? This was a time when drugs were still just coming onto the American scene. Our shock was heightened by the terrible stories we had heard about drug users—the life-threatening risks and the sullen attitude of rebellion. And I was a pastor, a leader in the church and community. What would our congregation say? Would the members still want me as pastor if I was a failure as a parent? Worst of all, had I failed Richard?

All of these questions raced through my mind in a matter of seconds before Johnnie and I both asked, "Richard, is this so?"

Very slowly he answered, looking alternately at the floor and at me, "Yes, sir."

At this point Bill excused himself and left our family to struggle with this new and devastating situation.

I waited a few minutes and then did the only thing I knew to do: I issued an ultimatum.

"Richard, you must promise to stop this now or you will have to leave home. We are a little society here and we cannot allow you to stay and deliberately break the law of the land, of this house and of God." Both Johnnie and I told him how much we loved him and we promised to do all we could to help him.

It seemed like a lifetime, but only a few minutes passed before Richard replied. "I can't promise you I'll break with my friends and quit drugs," he said, "so I guess I'll leave."

A scene followed that caused as much sorrow as I had ever known to that point in my life. Richard began moving all his belongings into his old car. By this time the whole family knew something very sad was happening. Everyone wept, even little John.

Personally I could not have been any sadder at that moment if an ambulance crew had been taking out my son's dead body. This was a living death. Fears filled my heart, and Johnnie's as well, as our imaginations ran wild.

Where was Richard going?

What would happen next?

What could we do?

As Richard's worn Plymouth pulled out of the driveway, a new day began at our house.

Johnnie Seeks God

Immediately after Richard left, Johnnie went into our bedroom. As she told me later, she cried out to God, "O Father, my son is gone! What shall I do?"

God is faithful and practical. He answered Johnnie's desperate cry by speaking these words to her heart: *You have a responsibility to teach Sunday school tomorrow. Do that and then come aside on Monday so we can spend time together.*

On Monday Johnnie packed her bags, informing me she would not be back until she had a word from God about the situation. She headed for a motel in Daytona Beach where she could be alone.

Johnnie had had a personal faith-crisis in the mid-1950s. The resulting nervous breakdown, caused by years of trying to live a Christian life beyond reproach in her own strength, had prepared her for this moment. Her encounters with God then and since had taught her that while she was weak, helpless and needy, Jesus Christ was adequate for the situation. She needed to hear from Him in order to know how to respond to Richard's needs. I knew these things, too, but not as experientially as Johnnie did then. She has always been light years ahead of me in this area of listening to—and obeying—the leading of the Holy Spirit. So I knew I could trust what God would say to her.

I will be returning to the details of Richard's story periodically throughout this book, along with stories of our other children, but I would like to stop here to discuss Johnnie's obedient action. It demonstrates several lessons both of us were learning in our personal walks of faith, lessons that are foundational for any parent who longs to hear a word from God about his or her children. We will see how these worked out through the course of this book.

1. She made Jesus her first choice. In times of crisis we need to make the Lord Jesus our first choice and not our last chance. We often try everything and everyone else and then in desperation go to Him. What does that say about the depth of our trust?

God is honored and exalted when we seek His advice and help first, not waiting until we exhaust all human means. Remember, He is the ultimate expert on our children, as well as on everything else in this world. And when we turn first to Him, we avoid the temptation to react out of shock and/or anger, which usually makes a bad situation worse.

2. She gave Him her full attention. Is it always necessary to pull aside as Johnnie did in order to hear God? No, but some situations are so grave they cannot be dealt with casually. We must be prepared to take whatever time and means are required to get a word from God on which to base our faith.

While it is true that we can contact our Lord in the midst of a busy schedule, sometimes we need to get away from it all. When we have crises in the physical and emotional realms we stop all regular activities until they are over. Why not do the same in the vital realm of the spiritual?

3. She didn't rush God. Sometimes God will not give an answer in fifteen minutes. Johnnie was learning she could not rush God, but must wait until He wanted to speak. Notice that God didn't instruct her to race around frantically, find a substitute for her Sunday school class and throw clothes into a suitcase so she could drive to the motel that Saturday night. And notice also that she did not necessarily expect Him to give her a word of faith regarding Richard within a specified amount of time. That is why she said, "I will not be back until He speaks to me in some way."

Our Father is not reluctant to help, but He knows we have a tendency to use Him, to get what we want and then leave Him until we need Him again. Using people is detrimental to any relationship and will lead ultimately to its deterioration and destruction. God desires fellowship with us. In fact, I believe that sometimes He does not answer right away because He just wants to spend time with us.

4. She let Him work on her, too. God often wants to deal with our part in a crisis, the things we *did* wrong because we *were* wrong. No situation is ever completely the fault of one person, and the sure way *not* to solve it is to place one hundred percent of the blame on the other party.

Our Lord wants to correct faulty thinking, heal damaged and destructive emotions, refresh our spirits and strengthen faith, hope and love in our lives, as well as answer the requests of our hearts. We will discuss this point more fully in chapter 3.

Getting a Word from God

You have probably noticed that Johnnie and I hear very clear and specific words from the Lord.

How do I get a word from God? How do I know His voice? People ask me these two questions more often than any other. That they even ask demonstrates how much we Christians in the West have to learn.

Why? Because for a Christian to hear God's voice easily and regularly should be a normal and natural occurrence. Jesus' most often repeated statement is "he who has ears to hear let him hear" (Matthew 11:15; Mark 4:9, 23; Luke 8:8). He also said, "My sheep hear My voice, and I know them, and they follow Me" (John 10:27). We can couple these verses with the fact that the Holy Spirit lives in each Christian for the purpose of communicating God's love and guidance. Hearing His voice is natural and normal for His people.

The Christian life is one of faith, but we can have no real faith for a particular parenting crisis until we have heard from God. Ninety percent of the parent-child dilemmas we face are not specifically addressed in Scripture except by way of broad guidelines and principles. It is always necessary, therefore, for us to go to God and ask for a word, a word we can stand on. We need the Holy Spirit to apply those broad guidelines to our individual situations.

It is my greatest joy to teach others to hear His voice. It is very easily done and I want to offer here two guidelines. You will note that they are nearly identical to the two crucial components for a profitable quiet time that we discussed in chapter 1. Just as they apply to our regular, daily times with God, so they apply when we need a word of faith for a specific parenting dilemma.

1. Get ready to hear. If you believe in Jesus Christ as your Savior and have asked Him to be the Lord of your life, accept by faith the following facts: God is your Father who loves you very much and has sent the Helper, the Holy Spirit, to live in you; as a Christian you have the capacity to hear Him speak to you or, as the Bible puts it, you have spiritual ears to hear (Ezekiel 12:2; Mark 7:16).

Remember: We receive spiritual communication through our minds. Getting ready to hear by meditating on Scripture, alone with God, allows the Holy Spirit to speak.

2. Pray. Praying includes listening as well as talking. Prayer is really a conversation with your heavenly Father.

We can be sure of this: God knows the pains of our hearts. He is not impressed by vain repetitions or much speaking (Matthew 6:7–8), but He is intensely interested in His children's sincere cries for help.

He wants us to desire Him for *Himself,* however, and not only for His blessings. When we get to the place where we can love and enjoy Him for Himself and not just for what He can do for us, He will give us more than we have sense to ask for.

So start by opening your heart to Him. Tell Him the burden you have for your wandering child and then listen. How can He speak unless you stop talking and give Him a chance?

God will always answer you. His answer may not be what you want or expect, but it will be the right place to begin dealing with your parent-child problem.*

Remember: The Scriptures always lead us to the living Word of God, Jesus, and to the *rhema,* or specific word of encouragement and instruction we need for a particular circumstance. Sometimes the Holy Spirit makes a certain verse of Scripture come alive, as if we had never seen it before. Sometimes He whispers a word based on some principle from the Bible. James writes in his epistle, "If any of you lacks wisdom, let him ask of God, who gives to all men generously and without reproach, and it will be given to him" (1:5). The Holy Spirit, we may be assured, will never lead us astray.

* For further reading in the area of communication with God, see *Hearing God* by Peter Lord (Baker Book House).

God's Word to Johnnie

As Johnnie got ready to hear, by going off to that Daytona Beach motel to spend time alone with God, and as she prayed, the Holy Spirit spoke in the quiet of her heart: *Richard is coming back, but I'm not going to tell you when or how.*

With this word of faith our journey began. As we prayed and cooperated with God toward its fulfillment, we faced many difficult days, but we had His promise to cling to.

Having received the word of faith, it was now time to enter the walk of faith. This means allowing Him to work with us as parents and is the subject of the next chapter.

3

The Walk of Faith

Principle: In the walk of faith God cleans up parents' lives as they wait and pray for His promises for their children to be fulfilled.

Scripture: Jeremiah 7:23; Psalm 138:7; Romans 4:12; 2 Corinthians 5:7

Faith always has a walk. Even though faith for our children's total well-being—physical, emotional, spiritual and mental—begins with a promise from God, there comes a time when we must act and react on the basis of that promise, and not on what we see happening in their lives.

Many parents, including me, find this difficult. We are impatient. We get discouraged by our children's behavior and the circumstances surrounding them and we want results from our prayers. But in the walk of faith, God teaches us patiently, situation by situation, that we have much to learn, too.

In his bestselling book *The Road Less Traveled*, M. Scott Peck makes the following statement:

> The neurotic assumes too much responsibility; the person with the character disorder not enough. When neurotics are in conflict with the world they automatically assume they are at fault. When those with character disorders are in conflict with the world they automatically assume that the world is at fault.

Most of us probably fit somewhere in the middle of these extremes. Sometimes we fall under the weight of our own guilt, feeling we have done everything wrong. Sometimes we strike out at the other person, blaming him or her entirely for causing so much pain.

From my own experience and observation I would say that in any conflict or trouble, including the heartbreak of having a child leave God, some of the problem lies on both sides. There is not much we can do about the other person: Trying to make someone over is an exercise in futility for anyone but God. But we can work with God to change ourselves. Here are two principles to help us.

God Gets Our Attention

Have you noticed that when the physical and material matters of life are going well, it is harder to stay in communion with God? The unfortunate reason for this is that Christians' value systems often differ little from those of non-Christians: We place far too much emphasis on the blessings of this world, and far too little on the richness of conforming to the image of Jesus Christ.

When problems come we turn to Him, true enough,

but if we could only realize that when we make our relationship with God our number one priority at all times, we have far fewer troubles.

There are two reasons for this. First, when we are meditating on Scripture and praying conversationally with God, He becomes our "high tower" (see 2 Samuel 22:3; Psalm 18:2; 144:2, KJV). He helps us see the enemy coming so that we can head off the attack. Second, our regular times alone with God keep us tuned to the voice of the Helper, the Holy Spirit. This means that we make far fewer errors of omission and commission.

We have a tendency, however, to take God for granted. And so, as a parent and through forty years of pastoring, I have learned this first principle: Our Lord often uses children's problems to get the attention of their busy, preoccupied parents. He desires good for us as well as for our children, and He is working on us as well as on them.

By now Johnnie and I have learned, when our children are troubled or in trouble, to ask God if He is trying to teach us something in the process. Since He has our full attention when we are concerned about a child, He is able to deal with us in any way He desires. If there is nothing in our attitudes, actions or reactions that needs correcting, He will tell us so. If there is, He can show us what to do about it.

Often we do not understand His ways any more than our children understand ours. Someone once said, "God is willing to look bad for the moment in order that over the long haul He may do good." And God Himself reminds us in Isaiah 55:8–9, " 'My thoughts are not your thoughts, neither are your ways My ways,' declares the Lord. 'For as the heavens are higher than the earth, so are My ways higher than your ways, and My thoughts than your thoughts.' "

God, What Are You Saying to Me?

Early one morning more than a dozen years ago, I was in my small study in our church where I go in the early hours to have my quiet time. While meditating on Scripture and praying for our nine-year-old, John, I learned a major lesson about God's using children's difficulties to accomplish His purposes in their parents' lives.

At this particular time I was spending two hours each day alone with God. One of my disciplines and joys was to read five Psalms a day.

But I had developed a bad habit from the period when I had simply studied God's Word and knew little about meditating on it: I skipped over portions of Scripture that seemed to hold no meaning for me or for anyone else I knew.

One verse that I skipped over easily appears twice in the Psalms. This means I came across it twice a month or 24 times a year. Found in Psalm 60:8 and again in Psalm 108:9, it says, "Moab is My washbowl; over Edom I shall throw My shoe; over Philistia I will shout aloud." This is not a verse we normally decoupage for our refrigerator doors!

That morning I saw this text coming up and was gaining speed to jump over it, when the Holy Spirit said to me, *Stop!*

Well, I did—right on "Moab is my washbowl."

Then the Holy Spirit said to me, *Get your Bible dictionary and look up Moab.* I learned that the Moabites were Israel's kinfolk who lived next door.

Then the Holy Spirit said, *Let Me explain this Scripture to you. When My people, Israel, got dirty, I used their wicked kinfolk to wash them up.*

I still remember my excitement at understanding an obscure verse that had been like a foreign language to me.

The Holy Spirit is much more, of course, than a history teacher. He is interested in our lives and wants to help us live them to the fullest. So He said to me, *Here is the application of this truth for you. You have been praying, asking Me to clean John up, but I am using him to clean you up.*

Wow! I had been handing God a list of things I wanted Him to do in John's life, but He was using John to clean *me* up, and still is, even though John has now been redeemed.

I like to compare this process to what happens when you shake a full glass of water. What comes out? Splashes of water. But the water does not slosh out just because we shake the glass; it comes out because it was already in there to begin with.

The same is true as our children's behavior and attitudes shake us. Out slosh our worry, fear, rejection, resentment, sarcasm and insecurity. That is not the children's fault: Those flaws were in there to begin with. God's cleansing happens when we acknowledge our need for Him to clean out our sin and inadequacies and replace them with the power and wisdom of His Holy Spirit.

This can take some time. Johnnie sometimes says to me, "Are we going to have to take this course again?" meaning, "When are we going to learn the lessons God is trying to teach us?"

You see, God does not give social promotions. He does not say, "Let's just forget about trying to teach Peter this lesson. It doesn't look like he wants to learn it, so let's just move him up to the next grade."

He loves us too much to do that. He is not content to leave those things in us that hurt us and prevent us from receiving and returning His love. When we fail to learn the lessons He tries to teach us, He works on us just that much longer.

As I reflected on the Holy Spirit's words to me that morning, I realized I needed to pray differently. I needed to ask Him not only for John's redemption, but also to help me cooperate as He did His work in me.

I went home that day singing and praising, as I always do when God speaks, because He is the great encourager.

Another Lesson

But God had another lesson to teach me about the walk of faith from this experience. Just a few minutes after I arrived back home that morning I was standing in front of the bathroom mirror shaving and getting ready for the day. I still felt as though I were bouncing on six inches of joy. Then a terrible thought flashed through my mind.

"Yes, John is going to be used to clean you up, but just as Moab went to hell, so will John."

That is not fair! I shouted in my heart. *That is not fair!*

Despite the many hours I had spent learning to hear God's voice, I assumed wrongly that God was speaking again. But that was not His voice. I did not realize then that when God speaks, the devil will often come and say something to distort what God has just said. He may challenge God's word to us, or deny it.

Then God really did speak again, and my heart responded with warm recognition, because this time the message was one of help and comfort, as God's messages always are. Even more thrilling, this time God had a word of faith for me—the first ever—about John's future salvation and relationship with Him.

God said, *Ruth was a Moabitess.* With those few words God refuted the enemy's lie in comparing our John's ultimate fate to that of the wicked Moabites. Ruth *was* a Moabitess, but God worked mightily in her life, and eventually she became a member of the house and lineage of David, a link in the ancestry of Jesus Christ.

Hallelujah! God had given me a strong promise to stand on! Not only would John be redeemed to be His child, but he would also be used in God's redemptive purposes, just as Ruth was.

But He had also taught me that morning that I need to be sure I am hearing *His* voice as we continue on the walk of faith.

Standing on the Promises

The second major principle God teaches us in the walk of faith is to stand on the promises He gives for our children, and not to stand (or base our feelings, attitudes and actions) on what they are doing and saying.

I wish I could tell you that I have learned this lesson once and for all, that I now stand consistently on God's promises despite what my children's outward behavior indicates, but I can't. When I take my eyes of faith off of God's promises and place them on individual behaviors I usually react out of anger and fear. Neither anger nor fear is of God. Both come from the evil one.

I am grateful that our heavenly Father is continuing to cleanse me of worry and fear in my life. He is teaching me to live by faith, to trust Him. He is showing me that faith is a walk based not on what I see, but on what He has said.

I recently read this statement of David Grant's: "If I treat you as though you were what you could become, that is what you *will* become."

What a powerful beacon of hope and truth for the parent trying to act on God's promise for a child!

The other day God asked me in my quiet time, *How do you see John today? Are you looking at his present, stabilized, but still uncommitted behavior? Or do you see him through the eyes of faith, as he will be when I completely fulfill the word of faith I gave you about him?*

Can you think how you would answer that question if the Holy Spirit asked you about your child? Can you trust Him to keep His word even when you can't see any changes? This is a critical challenge.

You see, one of God's methods in dealing with human beings is to work from the inside out. He may be working on the inside of your child or mine—in his character, in her heart. Since these are places and works we cannot see, we have no idea what is going on. In fact, there may be times when we see no outward conflict or rebellion and assume that all is well. We drop our guard and become careless about trusting God to continue His work. We forget that attitudes go bad inside before they show up on the outside.

If we concentrate on the outward appearance (see 1 Samuel 16:7), we will have wrong reactions. It follows that we will try to take matters into our own hands. This will hinder God's work.

It may help to remember that until there is a fundamental change on the inside there is really no change at all. Inside changes bring about a permanent work. The condition of the inner life always precedes the expression of the outer life.

But what do you do in the meantime when the outward behavior is appalling? I can just hear you asking the question! After all, you say, parents can't just ignore attitudes and actions while they wait for God to keep His promises!

No, but you can take them to God in prayer. You can ask God to help you learn what it is He wants to show you. In short, you can be patient. This is the walk of faith in which God deals with us. In the *work* of faith, which we will discuss in the next chapter, we will see how He helps us deal with the need for correction, discipline and instruction.

Some Tips for the Journey

God has individual lessons to teach each parent on the walk of faith. Johnnie's lessons were not for me, nor were mine for Johnnie. But we did pick up several tips that can apply to everyone.

1. Keep relationships strong. The devil likes to lure us into neglecting our relationships with God and our families. His plan is to separate us from God and each other and to make us spiritually weak. Then when he launches a major attack, we are unable to resist in a Christlike way. Our ungodly reactions and/or strained relations make bad situations worse. Estranged from grace, and weak in faith and love, we do not respond as a follower of Jesus should.

I remember hearing Pastor Paul Yonggi Cho, of the famous Full Gospel church in Korea, tell how he became so involved in ministry that his personal relationship with God deteriorated. One day during a meeting he received a message that his son was dying of food poisoning. He rushed home and began to pray, only to find how far he had drifted from a close and dynamic relationship with God. It took him six hours of concentration and confession to get back in tune with the Lord Jesus and be able to pray effectively for his son.

So beware! When you sense in your spirit that you are drifting from God or your family, take action. Restore the "ties that bind" no matter what it takes so that the devil cannot capitalize on your weakness.

2. Pray out of faith, not fear. Fear drives us, and driven people are too caught up in their own inner turmoil to relate to God.

When we confronted Richard about his drug use and he chose to move out of our home, we were scared, scared stiff about what could happen to him. He was gone: That was bad. *Where* he had gone—to live with a group of hippies—was worse!

But once Johnnie received the word of faith about Richard, we had to learn to pray out of faith, not fear.

I remember, for example, that after Richard left home I prayed repeatedly, "Father, do anything to Richard to bring him back except put him in jail."

One day, when I let Him, God said to me, *Why don't you want him in jail?*

I gave what I thought was the obvious answer. "Father, it would ruin his life!"

To my surprise God asked again, *Why don't you want him in jail?*

Now I know that when God asks a question a second time it is not because He did not hear my first answer, but because my first answer was a lie. So I examined my response and said, "Well, to tell You the truth, if Richard ended up in jail his name would be in the papers. We live in a small town and people in the world love to publish anything bad about ministers and the Church. Then what would they think about us?"

God answered kindly, *You see, your problem is one of pride.* And I realized that I was less concerned about how jail would affect Richard's life than I was fearful of having my name dragged through the dust.

Fear blocks us from seeing the root issues God needs to deal with. When we learn to abandon fear and pray out of faith, the Holy Spirit is able to deal with the root issues, and His work can continue.

3. Don't hide your problems out of pride. In years of helping people with family problems I have observed that one of the first things they want a pastor to promise is that he or she won't "tell anybody." Well-trained pastors, of course, always maintain confidentiality; that is not the issue here. The issue is that we humans like to hide our problems to protect our pride. And pride, like fear, always blocks relationships.

Johnnie and I are fortunate because God has given us a congregation that allows us to take off our masks. We can tell them when and where and how we are hurting, and know that they will not use our problem against us, but rather will pray and support us.

This is not to say you should broadcast your difficulties with your children to anyone and everyone. But sharing with a pastor and close friends at church, or a support group, opens the way for the Holy Spirit to speak through them to you. In addition, the lessons the Holy Spirit teaches you may bless someone else.

The principles that help light the walk of faith are not always easy, but that does not negate the fact that God loves both parents and children with a tender, patient love. And He helps us express that love to others, too.

Throughout that spring of 1971 and on into 1972, Richard was on drugs and not giving a single indication that he wanted to change. But Johnnie and I had received a word of faith from our heavenly Father that someday Richard would be fine—fine from God's viewpoint and value system—and we would not let go.

God was also using the situation to get our attention and bring us to greater Christian maturity, correcting our faults and giving us a deeper understanding of Himself and how to relate to Him. As we trusted Him on the walk of faith, His presence and teaching sweetened even the bitter pill of watching our child stray.

Now it was time to enter the work of faith.

4

The Work of Faith

Principle: In the work of faith, God asks us to cooperate with Him, step by step, as He deals with our children's sins, problems and potential.

Scripture: James 2:14, 17, 18

In the first chapter of this book we talked about two building blocks on which the whole volume rests—*relating intimately to God* through prayer and meditation and *cooperating with God.*

Johnnie and I were accepting the *word* of faith and attempting the *walk* of faith. But we were also learning that God usually asks parents to cooperate with Him in solving difficult parent-child situations, and that is the *work* of faith. So we were asking for and receiving instructions from Him about what He wanted us to do with Richard.

This has a sound biblical basis. There are numerous stories in the Bible in which men and women were required to cooperate with God in order to see His promises come true.

Remember, after receiving God's promise:

- by faith Noah obeyed God and built an ark (Genesis 6);
- by faith Abram obeyed God and left his hometown of Haran, moving to a land he did not know (Genesis 12);
- by faith Naaman, afflicted with leprosy, obeyed Elisha and dipped in the Jordan River seven times (2 Kings 5);
- by faith the blind man obeyed Jesus and washed in the pool of Siloam (John 9:1–7).

I could go on and on, listing incident after incident in which God asked His children to act on His instructions in order to receive the fulfillment of His promise. We are His children in this generation, and the principle is just as true for us today as it was in Bible times.

There may be times when you wish God would just do an overnight miracle. Believe it or not, that might not draw you closer to Him. We are quick to forget God's goodness, or to take it for granted. In asking us to cooperate with Him, God leads us into more intimate dependency on and fellowship with Himself, and also grants us the joy and satisfaction of being part of the solution.

Let's look now at ten principles God taught Johnnie and me about the work of faith.

1. Faith is always a choice. I often hear a person say, "Well, I have no choice but to believe," and think that is faith. It isn't. Faith always involves the choice to trust God and His Word or something or someone else—including yourself.

Wait a minute, Peter! you say. We've already received the word of faith for our wandering child, and we're trying to allow God to deal with our own problems on the walk of faith as we wait for the promise to be fulfilled. Why this reminder that faith is a choice? We *have* faith!

For some reason God doesn't seem to give His children a lifelong dose of faith all at once. He could. He could say, "Here, Peter, you'll need this much. Here, Johnnie, you'll need this much. That ought to last you until you get to heaven."

No, God seems instead to want us to choose to appropriate the faith we need for each new situation. When we do, He's not stingy; He comes more than halfway to meet us.

"Lord, I believe; help my unbelief," the father of a tormented child once said to Jesus. Did Jesus scold him for his unbelief? No, He tenderly fulfilled His promise and healed the child (Mark 9:14–27).

God is pleased when we choose to exercise our faith. And since our faith grows each time we do, it becomes a little bit easier to appropriate it the next time.

We need to reaffirm our trust in God during each encounter with our children because then we are admitting that He is the One who acts on our behalf, and we are less tempted to take credit ourselves for His work. When we choose, by faith, to believe that He knows best and try to cooperate with Him, each victory, no matter how small, belongs to Him.

2. We need to take it step by step. This business of cooperating with God in the work of faith is a step-by-step procedure. Leading us one step at a time seems to be God's normal method, even though we often wish He would unfold His entire plan at once.

There are at least two reasons for His dealing with us this way. First, it is our human tendency to take His blessings for granted. If we know only one step at a time, we are forced to depend on Him, to relate intimately to Him, to go back to Him day after day to give thanks for what has occurred in the lives of our children, and to receive encouragement and instruction to go on.

Second, if God showed us a blueprint of the future, we would do one of two things. We might take it and run, trying to accomplish our children's salvation and deeper walk with God all on our own. Or we might shrink in fear from what is ahead for our children, our families and ourselves before the promise is fulfilled, and refuse to keep walking in faith.

3. We need to remember that we are not responsible for changing our chidren. Only God can change a person—fundamentally, deep down, restructuring even his or her natural inclinations. This is another way of saying what I said earlier: Our *actions* cannot make a child godly; only *God* can make a child godly.

You see, we function best when we are doing what comes naturally. The Christian life is not meant to be a continual struggle to be something we are not. God alone can give each of us a new quality of life—through salvation and redemption by Jesus Christ and by the power of the indwelling Holy Spirit—and develop it so that it flows naturally.

Our responsibility to our children, therefore, is not to change them, but to train them to live in the world. We will develop this point in more detail in chapter 8.

4. We can adopt an open-door policy. One of the ways God told us to cooperate with Him about Richard was to tell our son that our door was always open to him: He could come home and visit as often as he liked. And he did—to wash clothes and eat! Naturally, these visits gave us opportunities to talk with him.

We soon realized—and this is why I include the open-door policy as a principle—that since Richard wanted nothing to do with Christians or the Church, we were the only direct and personal contact God would have with him through people. It was important for us to make the most of these contacts by allowing him to see Christ in us. The open-door policy showed him that while we did not approve of his lifestyle, we loved him and had not rejected him.

I know from our own experiences that it is easy in the strain of parent-child confrontations to move in anger or hopelessness and decide to wash your hands of the whole matter: "Just get out and leave this family in peace!"

Remember two things: 1) Both temper and hopelessness are not from God. They are from the devil. Leash your anger and go to God in your quiet time for instructions before acting. 2) You may be the last human contact through whom God can manifest His love to your child. Don't shut the door unless the Lord gives specific directives to do so—and this would be the exception, not the rule.

5. We need to make our children responsible for the consequences of their choices. We do our children no favors when we soften the consequences of their rebellious behavior. If we have cooperated with God (acting on the Holy Spirit's directions or impressions) by setting consequences for a certain act, we must continue to cooperate by following through, whether the child is age two or twenty. In fact, the earlier we parents learn this principle, and the earlier the child knows we have learned it and sees us acting on it, the easier life will be for everyone!

As I indicated in chapter 1, I had told Richard that if he got arrested for his drug use we were not going to bail him out. "Make sure you are prepared to live with the consequences of your choices," I had said.

Soon after our conversation came the telephone call telling us Richard had, indeed, been arrested for possession of narcotics and was being held in Orlando until he could be arraigned. As you can imagine, cooperating with God was not easy for either Johnnie or me. God had to strengthen our backbones to enable us to leave

Richard in that jail—and He did. It was probably one of the best, and toughest, learning experiences Richard had. It certainly made a memorable impression on us.* We will address this topic further in chapter 15, "Knowing Where to Draw the Lines."

6. We must not react to our children's behavior but should allow the Holy Spirit to determine our responses. I have touched on this idea briefly, but it is important to look at it further. Some of my greatest mistakes as a parent have come from reacting to my children's actions. I have allowed their behavior to determine my response—and my response was usually anger.

Here is an important distinction to help you understand this principle of cooperating with God: Reactive behavior responds instantly, like a knee-jerk reflex, rather than taking the time to consider the matter from a deep, internal value system.

What if God had responded reactively to man's sin and rebellion in Noah's time? Rather than take elaborate measures to save Noah and his family from the flood in order to repopulate the earth, He could have wiped out humankind forever in one angry stroke. He chose instead to give us a second chance, and sent Jesus to redeem and reconcile willing members of the human race to intimate relationship with Him. He did that out

* For further ideas in this area I recommend *Dare to Discipline* and *The Strong-Willed Child,* both by Dr. James Dobson, and *How to Make Your Children Mind Without Losing Yours* by Dr. Kevin Leman.

of His deep, internal value system of love and compassion and commitment.

If, by the grace of God, we hear from Him regularly and live by His principles and His value system, we, too, can respond to our children's behavior out of love, compassion and commitment.

We need to acknowledge that our knee-jerk reactions often arise out of fear. "Why in the world did you *do* that? Don't you realize how seriously you could have been hurt?"

When we forget to exercise our faith for each situation, fear takes over. And fear always brings a reactive response. But when we choose to trust God with the details of our response, He helps us to avoid the internally and externally destructive consequences of fear.

7. It is important to be honest, not devious, about our labors. Christians are tempted far too often to use deceptive methods in order to get someone to hear the Gospel.

You would be surprised how many times a Christian husband or wife or mother or father with an unbelieving loved one has said to me, "My spouse/child is home tonight. Why don't you just drop in? He will never invite you or let me invite you."

I do not agree with this method. The end does not justify the means. We need to be open—not obnoxiously, but courteously—about our spiritual concern for a loved one.

Johnnie and I discovered how God will bless our use

of this principle. After Richard got out of jail we felt our Father instructing us to invite Richard and all his friends to our house for a meal with the express purpose of sharing with them a different way of life—God's way.

So I went to the house where about eight of them were living. I remember standing on the front porch and saying to them, "You fellows can see from your recent arrest that you are heading for trouble. We would like to have you over for a meal and explain to you about an alternate lifestyle."

Miraculously, they accepted. I use the word *miraculous* because that was how it seemed from our perspective. Why were they willing to visit us when they knew that Richard's father was a Christian pastor and that the alternate lifestyle he was proposing was undoubtedly Christianity?

But when we ask God for instructions and He gives them, we can be sure He has a plan. One of the obvious reasons they accepted, of course, was the prospect of a free meal! Richard had shared with us on one of his visits that all of their money went for drugs, and food was scarce. God wasn't reluctant to use their need to draw them toward Him. So their acceptance wasn't any miracle from His viewpoint; it was just His way of accomplishing His work.

After the boys had eaten the lovely dinner Johnnie prepared for them, I shared the Gospel. They listened politely. Then I said, "Would any of you like to receive Jesus as Lord and Savior and start a new life?" Much to my surprise a young man sitting at the end of the table said, "I would." Then and there Buzzy prayed to receive Christ and become one of His followers. Shortly afterward the boys left.

Devious methods to "corner" our children with the Gospel may backfire, appearing to them not as acts of genuine love and commitment, but as a desire to "add scalps" to our belts. But if we cooperate with the Holy Spirit in expressing our spiritual concerns for them *as He directs us to,* our Father will continue to work in them.

8. We need to give of ourselves generously. You may be sure that God is working out His plan to fulfill the word of faith He gave concerning your child. But watch out! It is far too easy to want God to do all of the work while we just continue on as before. In many instances He wants to use us, His servants, to perform His will.

We found this out in a surprising way. A few days after Richard and his friends ate dinner with us there was a knock at our front door. I answered it and there was Buzzy.

"Mr. Lord," he said, "I can't live the Christian life in the place where I am staying now. Can I come and live with you?"

Wow! This would require quite a commitment from Johnnie and me. But as soon as we considered Buzzy's request we realized his dilemma, and agreed gladly to take him in and disciple him in the ways of the Lord Jesus.

It was not an easy commitment for a busy pastor's family to make. But we were soon doubly glad we had: When Buzzy moved in with us, Richard came, too. We had never known they were best friends.

Buzzy kept growing in the Spirit and continued to follow Jesus, active in a church and in Kingdom work until his untimely death in a construction accident. How grateful we were to know that God had used us to bring that young man into the Kingdom! We were thankful that we had been willing to cooperate with God in sharing ourselves, our home and our family time with Buzzy.

Richard remained unchanged at this point except that he did not use drugs at home. He lied about his drug use elsewhere, but he was home, and exposed to a Christian atmosphere. Praise God! He works all things together for good—even our rebellious children's "unsavory" friends!

9. We must uphold Christian standards and practices in the home as "givens." It is my firm conviction that God has given parents the privilege and responsibility of educating our children in the Christian faith. That task does not belong to the local church or the Christian school, although they may serve supportive roles. (There are times, however, when God allows a church or Christian school to play a major role in a child's life, such as when the parents are not Christians.)

When we do our part by modeling a Christian lifestyle and educating our children in the faith—through devotional times or "family altar," Christian music, books and exposure to other Christians and Christian experiences—we release God to change their hearts and form them into godly people.

It is important for children to understand that certain of these practices are "givens" in the home. They are non-negotiable: Everyone is to participate. (Parents may need, as the children grow older, to make individual judgment calls as to which practices are negotiable, and at what ages. Here is another area where the Holy Spirit can give you discernment.)

Naturally we need to do our best to be somewhat flexible in planning the schedule, so as to make it possible for family members to take part, and to make the activities enjoyable and oriented to the age levels and abilities of the children involved.

We always had family altar times with our children as they were growing up. Since John was younger than the last of our other four youngsters by about nine years, there were several years after the older ones left when he was virtually an only child. Morning after morning Johnnie and I had devotions with him, but it was one of the hardest things I have ever done. Even before his time of rebellion he was not really interested. During his rebellion he said, "I do not want anything to do with God or the Church. I do not care about any of that stuff." I persisted in having devotions with him, but it was terrible. He seldom paid attention, and frequently fell asleep.

But what I did, I did by the firm conviction that God wanted me to do it. I knew He could and would use the facts and principles I was teaching during those devotional times as soon as John was ready to incorporate them into his life.*

10. We need to be willing, as God directs, to ask for our children's forgiveness. I have become a professional in asking forgiveness from my children! I have failed them often, usually because I didn't seek God's direction for my responses, and reacted emotionally on the spot.

I just described how John often acted during our devotional times together. Can you guess how I reacted? By getting angry, over and over again. What a shame: Getting angry while seeking to impart the things of God! I learned, of course, that this was counterproductive; as James tells us, "The anger of man does not achieve the righteousness of God" (1:20). And so I would always apologize for the anger and its expressions.

Clearing the decks of hurts and wounds, both real and imagined, shows our children that we are still learners in the faith, too, and demonstrates our sincerity about living the walk we talk about so much.

I hope that these ten points will help you if you are

* For an excellent resource on Christian parents' responsibility to educate their children in the faith, see Sally Leman Chall's book *Making God Real to Your Children* (Fleming H. Revell Company).

currently struggling through the work of faith. My experience has been and still is that God rewards our faithful efforts. And even if we make many mistakes, He can redeem them, for He remembers our frame, that we are but dust (Psalm 103:14).

5

The Wait of Faith

Principle: The time between receiving the word of faith about a wandering child (a promise) and receiving its fulfillment is the wait of faith.

Scripture: Hebrews 11:1; Philippians 1:6

Faith always has a wait! That is the very nature of faith: If there were nothing to wait for, then we would have the fulfillment in our hands already. Hebrews 11:1 is, of course, the "classic" statement of this truth: "Faith is the assurance of things *hoped for*, the evidence of things *not seen*" (italics mine).

When the word of faith comes, it is usually a mountaintop experience. We sing and praise God because He has reassured us that He will answer our prayers and draw our erring children back to Himself.

But the wait of faith is done in the valleys of life, where the demoniacs live, as Jesus' disciples discovered when they came off the Mount of Transfiguration (Matthew 17; Mark 9). The wait of faith occurs as we live our everyday lives—with or without our children.

Personally I have found this to be the most difficult of all the aspects of faith. My fleshly nature is very impatient. It is a besetting sin of mine, an area of real weakness, one that I am working on, and in which God is working on me.

But most of us have only to look down the street or in our local newspapers to realize that our society as a whole is impatient. We demand "instant everything," from food to sex to money. A young mother from the city recently took her little girl to a Christian camp for a mother-daughter retreat. En route to the camp's rural location the mother was heard to exclaim, "I haven't seen a McDonald's for miles. My kids couldn't *live* without McDonald's!"

Her kids aren't alone. And our Western preoccupation with "having it all" and having it now has a drastic impact on our Christian faith.

Why Is God So Slow?

The wait of faith has been difficult to bear as God has worked on each of our children, but it has been longest (over eight years) and perhaps most difficult (who can qualify this type of thing?) in the life of our youngest son, John, whom I mentioned in the last chapter.

It almost never seems to fail that after you get a word from God about your child, a word on which to stand, a word of hope, the situation seems to get worse. In her absolutely delightful book *Pain Is Inevitable, Misery Is*

Optional, So Stick a Geranium in Your Hat and Be Happy, Barbara Johnson has entitled one chapter "It Is Always Darkest Just Before It Goes Totally Black."

In our parental experience, especially with John, this has been par for the course. It has seemed as if when things could not get worse, they did. We would think, *This is the fulfillment,* and then John would have a setback.

After a major turnaround in his spiritual life, John went off to college. This victory was followed, however, by a crisis in which he spent six months in a drug and alcohol recovery center and then six more months in a halfway house in Orlando. At this writing he is attending a Christian college. He is on the right track, more stabilized, but still with much to learn (like all of us!) in his personal relationship with Jesus.

Why is God so slow? Why does He take so long to fulfill His promises? Why, since He has the power to do anything, does He not do it right away, or at least more quickly, and save us all the pain and trouble?

Let me share with you four principles I believe God wants us to learn in the wait of faith.

1. God's concept of time is different from ours. I'll go even further: God's concept of time differs from ours completely! Peter's second letter tells us, "With the Lord one day is as a thousand years, and a thousand years as one day" (3:8).

Dr. Edward J. Willett, now retired after teaching economics at Houghton College for more than twenty years, uses an analogy from the days of the lower-flying piston-engine planes to explain God's concept of time. It was easy, back then, to see what was happening on the ground below.

One day as he was flying to Syracuse, New York, Dr. Willett saw a winding two-lane road below the plane, with two lines of cars heading toward each other, about a mile or so apart. The driver of a sports car, impatient to pass the leader of his line, kept pulling out to pass and dropping back, pulling out and dropping back. Apparently the road was so curvy he didn't dare go around the cars ahead of him.

"The thing that struck me," Dr. Willett says, "was that from my position in the plane, three thousand feet up, I could tell that if that sports car driver *did* pull out to pass he would almost certainly crash head-on into a car in the opposing lane. And that's how God must feel about me. Just as I could see the entire span of that highway and all the traffic on it, God can see the entire span of my life, past, present and future. But like the sports car driver, I can only see a short way ahead—a few days or weeks, at most. Once we begin to figure out that God sees the whole picture, and have faith that He is operating according to His perspective, we can better handle what life throws at us."

When God speaks a promise, He is speaking from His time perspective, not ours. The Bible says that "God is . . . a very present help in trouble" (Psalm 46:1). Not a past help, not a future help—a *present* help. I have learned that God may be very, very slow, but He is never, ever late!

2. God has bigger, better plans than we know enough to ask for. Remember Isaiah 55:8–9? " 'For My thoughts are not your thoughts, neither are your ways My ways,' declares the Lord. 'For as the heavens are higher than the earth, so are My ways higher than your ways, and My thoughts than your thoughts.' "

God's purposes in the wait of faith include much more than our requests that He redeem our children and draw them closer to Himself. (And even in fulfilling those requests, He outdoes Himself, going "exceeding abundantly beyond all that we ask or think" (Ephesians 3:20).) Our experience with Buzzy, told in the last chapter, is one example.

In our bedroom, where Johnnie and I pray together, hangs a banner of what we call the mission statement for our lives, our common goal: *Come worship the Lord with me and let us exalt His name together.* We also have a well-established family tradition that when we finish our prayer times we raise our hands over our heads and say, "The only reason we are alive is to glorify God."

It took me some time to see that God was not only allowing the trials with our children, but was using them, as a means to accomplish this desire in our lives.

Now we really hoped and prayed, of course, that God would conform us to His image painlessly, instantly, without cost to us. This has not happened and I don't think it will for us or for any of His children.

Through our children God has gained our attention and enabled us to make the character changes necessary in order for our lives to glorify Him.

Remember: It is always God's purpose to enlarge us so He can give us more, to develop us so He can trust us with more. If we cooperate with Him in the walk and wait of faith, acknowledging that His ways and thoughts are higher and wiser and better than ours, we will see someday just what He was trying to do.

3. The wait teaches us that we need others in the Body of Christ to support us. The wait of faith is best done in conjunction with other Christians. We need close friends to help us through those difficult times when things seem to be getting worse from every conceivable viewpoint.

As I mentioned earlier, most of us are tempted to hide our family problems in order to preserve an image of religious integrity. Such pride, plain and simple, not only displeases God because it denies our need for Him, but also robs us of the tremendous caring, camaraderie and lessons to be learned from other Christians who have themselves ached over wandering children.

If it were not for the wait of faith, we might never know the comfort that comes from feeling our burdens lift as our brothers and sisters in the Body join us in loving, praying and believing for our children.

4. The wait purifies our faith. It is easy to think that our faith is solid when we are talking about it or singing about it at church, but in the walk and wait of everyday life, in the valleys, we see how strong or weak, pure or flawed our faith really is.

You see, the plain teaching of Scripture is that faith pleases God and releases Him to act on our behalf (Hebrews 11:6). And a strong, pure faith carries with it an absolute assurance that God will keep His word (Hebrews 10:35; 11:1). So having faith is like knowing beyond the shadow of a doubt that your team is going to win. Even if you are so far behind at half time that a win seems impossible, you rejoice anyway.

But sometimes it seems we just can't. In those cases our faith in His promise is flawed. Adrian Rogers once said, "The faith that falters before the finish had a flaw in it from the first."

Among the many signs of flawed faith are despondency, worry, anger and depression. The best way to detect flawed faith is to listen to your own words. Make a list of all the things you say regularly about the problem (or the problem child) for whom God has given you a word of faith. Words are always indicators of the true heart condition because Jesus said, "Out of the abundance of the heart the mouth speaks" (Matthew 12:34; Luke 6:45).

Some time ago I went out to lunch with one of my children for whom I was at the time in the wait of faith. In the course of our conversation I asked him several questions. His answers indicated no change in some fundamental areas of his life, areas necessary not only for walking with God but for living life successfully on this planet.

Instead of turning to the Lord and asking Him to

reconfirm His promise and give me encouragement, I centered on the appearance of things and became discouraged and depressed. I did not respond to my son as a father with a strong, pure faith in God, but as a father who had no faith that his child was going to be redeemed. A meeting that should have been a positive encounter of love, mercy and grace turned instead into a temporary setback in our relationship. The experience left me in total despair and frustration.

When I got home I heard myself saying to Johnnie, "What's the use? I give up; I'm tired of trying. That child will never change. If God wants to act then He will, but our child shows no visible interest. I refuse to do any more; I wash my hands of this situation."

Later, as I rehearsed both my conversations with my child and with Johnnie, listening particularly to my own words of unbelief in God and His promise, I was appalled that I could have uttered such things. They were blasphemous expressions, attacks on the character of God. You can be sure I repented, but I also saw how flawed and imperfect my trust in God for this situation really was.

Even as our faith's flaws can be seen most easily in the way we talk, so can its strengths. True faith speaks confidently, joyously, thankfully. It sees and knows the end and is fully persuaded that what God has promised, He is able to perform. The repeated admonition from Scripture, "Let us not lose heart in doing good, for in due time we shall reap if we do not grow weary,"

(Galatians 6:9; 2 Thessalonians 3:13), is applicable both for the walk of faith and the wait of faith. God will fulfill the promises He has given concerning your children and mine. In the process He shows us how much refining our faith really needs.

6

The Fulfillment of Faith

Principle: The fulfillment of faith is when the word of faith—God's promise for the salvation and redemption of the wandering child—becomes flesh and blood reality.

Scripture: Hebrews 6:11–20

Suddenly . . . One Sunday night Richard was tripping out on LSD. The next Sunday night he was turned around and headed in a new direction—God's direction. The fulfillment of faith had come in Richard's life, and he has stayed on God's course now for twenty years.

Suddenly . . . One week John was in active rebellion, away from home, doing his own thing. By the next Sunday he was back home, after giving his life to Christ, confessing to and making restitution for crimes he had helped commit.

Suddenly . . . One week your son or daughter is wandering far from God, angry and disrespectful and selfish. The next week he or she has repented, received Christ as Savior and Lord, and is eagerly telling others about God's goodness.

Over and over again in this walk of faith, the fulfillment comes suddenly. Suddenly from our viewpoint and perspective, that is, but not from God's. It's all a part of the plan He has worked on all along. Through all of what *we* saw as ups and downs, starts and stops, progress and setbacks, He has been setting the stage for a visible manifestation of His work, the fulfillment of His word of faith to us.

God's ways are *not* our ways (Isaiah 55:8–9), a marvelous truth of which we need to be reminded over and over. So often we are like the children of Israel, who, according to the psalmist, "saw His works, but [did] not understand His ways" and therefore were unable to cooperate with Him. Sooner or later, in the walk and wait and through the work of faith, we discover the enormity of God's ways and plans and are glad to accept them as best.

I remember saying to Him, "God, if I were You I would do things much differently!"

He replied, *Look at the way you have done them. That's why they're in the mess they are now!* That was enough to stop my complaining!

As our years of parenting continue (for we never stop being parents) I keep on learning about the processes we have discussed in the last five chapters. I know now to seek a word of faith from Him for each of my children's difficulties. I try to allow Him freedom to deal with my sins on the walk of faith. I yield, sometimes fearfully, to His plan for correcting and redeeming my children for Himself in the work of faith. And I allow Him, sometimes hesitantly and unwillingly, to purify my trust in Him in the wait of faith.

Though I am stubborn and impatient and sometimes slow to learn, the process has always been sweetened by His love and mercy. And when the fulfillment of faith comes, that is truly a time of excitement. When God's word becomes reality and we see tangible answers to our heart's cries for our children, then we experience worship and wonder. Kneeling before our Lord and God, our Maker, we offer Him our thanksgiving, love, adoration and praise.

Thus far we have looked at the overall process through which we pass on the parent-child journey, from grieving parent and wandering child to rejoicing parent and redeemed child. Now, by studying the Fatherhood of God and His patterns for parenting, we can cultivate many attitudes and actions along the way that will help us cooperate more fully with God. Those patterns will be our focus in Section 2.

Section 2

God's Patterns for Parenting

7

The Heavenly Father, Our Model

The Bible refers over and over again to the tremendous Fatherhood of God, and to His watchcare over His children. I cannot say strongly enough that this is an area in which we need to study and meditate carefully, both as individuals and as the Church at large.

Students of human behavior—psychologists, teachers, psychiatrists, social workers, ministers, sociologists, to name just a few—have known for a long time that parental behavior affects children. In the last few years more and more books and articles have explored just how strongly those beliefs and attitudes shape children's feelings, actions and personalities.

And, yes, in Christian circles many sermons have been preached and some articles and books written, especially in recent years, on the connection between a child's relationship with his earthly father and his relationship with his heavenly Father. But not nearly enough thought has been given to just what kind of heavenly Father we have, or to the implications of His Fatherhood in straightening out the damaged places in our lives, or to the fact that He means for us to model ourselves as parents after Him.

Certainly neither Christians nor non-Christians have, by and large, taken seriously the knowledge and information now available about the crucial effect of parental modeling. If we were incorporating these understandings into our personal lives in any significant way, the impact on society—on crime rates and domestic satisfaction and educational statistics alone, not to mention on church life—would be noticeable within a few years. But such personal application requires changes in lifestyle and attitudes few of us are willing to make.*

Walter Brown Knight writes, "A father was one day teaching his little boy what manner of man a Christian is. When the lesson was finished, the father got the stab of his life when the boy asked, "Father, have I ever seen a Christian?"

Have our children ever seen Christians? Christian fathers and mothers whose parenting consistently resembles God's?

Hundreds of biblical passages show us the principles by which God operates as our Father, as you can see by

* For helpful reading about the earthly father/heavenly Father connection, see Donald Joy's *Becoming a Man* (Regal Books). Also, *Always Daddy's Girl* by H. Norman Wright (Regal Books).

checking any good-sized concordance. Just as an earthly parent has many roles to play in the lives of his children, so our heavenly Father plays many roles in our lives, including protector, nourisher, chastener, comforter, deliverer. We need to study and meditate on how God acted with and spoke to His children in the past, and how He continues to model the same fatherly attributes toward us, His children in this generation.

Just follow the Israelites on their journey to the Promised Land, for example, as told in the book of Exodus. God *heard* His children's cries of distress as they endured slavery (Exodus 2:24; 3:7–10). He promised to *be* with them (3:12–22). He *protected* them (11:5–7; 14). He *instructed* and *encouraged* them (14:2, 13–14). He *provided* for their physical nourishment (15:22–27; 16:11–21). He *rebuked* them (16:28). And all of this before they had been on the road two months!

Surely the God who inspired His servants to record such a wealth of interaction between Himself and His children wanted us to learn how to parent from His example.

The following chapters are an attempt to share several of God's patterns for parenting that Johnnie and I have discerned through trial and error, experience and the study of God's Word, our years of child-rearing and continuing to relate to our grown children. Again, it is important to remember that the Holy Spirit must interpret the application of these patterns to each of us individually for use with each of our children.

As we begin this all-too-brief study of how our Father's attributes need to be lived out in our dealings with our children, let us do so in the attitude of Walter Russell Bowie's thoughtful prayer, taken from his book *Lift Up Your Hearts*:

O God, who art our Father, take my human fatherhood and bless it with Thy Spirit. Let me not fail this little son of mine. Help me to know what Thou wouldst make of him, and use me to help and bless him. Make me loving and understanding, cheerful and patient and sensitive to all his needs so that he may trust me enough to come close to me and let me come very close to him. Make me ashamed to demand of him what I do not demand of myself; but help me more and more to try to be the kind of man that he might pattern himself after. And this I ask in the name and by the grace of Christ. Amen.

8

Cooperating with God

In the very first chapter of this book we concluded that the process of child-rearing is not applying a formula in order to build a product, but rather participating in the growth of a life that already contains predetermined qualities.

Now, as we work and pray our way through the five faith steps outlined in the first section of this book and learn more about God as our example of what a parent should be, we will find that He is changing our attitudes. He is shifting our gaze off the problem child and onto Himself as the solution. He is taking away our unrealistic expectations and helping us put our hope in Him. In other words, He is teaching us to cooperate with Him.

We know the concept of cooperation; now let's see how to put it into action. In this chapter we will study the patterns behind three key areas of cooperation: development, leaving change to God and training. The better our ability to apply ourselves to them, the better we will fall in step with God as He does the work of faith in a wayward child.

Development

For any living thing to develop, it must have two things: cooperation from the grower (provision of food, water and cultivation) and time.

When our first child was born, I was plowing and cultivating peanuts for a living on a farm in central Florida. It was long, hard work—especially the cultivating. I worked for ten to twelve hours a day on a tractor and could weed four rows at a time.

Eighteen years later, after our youngest was born, we revisited the same farm. The owners were still growing peanuts on the same property, but they were harvesting twice as many peanuts with about half the effort.

What had happened? The owners of that farm had learned better methods of cooperating with the life and growth process of the peanut plant.

Just as the farmer does not create the peanuts, so parents do not create a child's life; through the act of procreation we, the developers or growers, cooperate with God in creating it. Then we work to bring it to adulthood. Proper development encourages the child's greatest potential. A lack in this area can inhibit or even destroy life.

Any counselor, secular or religious, can tell you that a great number of the people he or she sees are unhappy in their vocations. They spend their lives doing what they are not fitted for, emotionally, physically or mentally, and therefore do not enjoy it.

This problem could have innumerable roots, but I would venture to say that a good portion of them are traceable to parents who did not cooperate with the child's natural development.

Take, for just one instance, the parents who ship children off to college who are totally ill-equipped for that experience. Perhaps they are gifted in working with their hands and would find personal satisfaction in studying at a trade school.

It isn't hard to see that the children's inevitable unhappiness has been caused by parents who tried to get them to do things they were not designed to do. In other words, the parents tried to build certain traits into their children, rather than helping develop what was there inherently.

A story in the popular children's book series *Frog and Toad* illustrates the concept of time. It tells how Toad wanted to have a garden. He planted seeds and watered them but was dismayed when they didn't sprout within a few hours!

As ridiculous as Toad's ignorance may seem to us, that is sometimes how we parents treat our children's development process. We want instant results. We overlook the fact that each life-form has a time for growth scheduled into its being at conception.

This is true in the natural realm; children develop different abilities at different stages and at their own paces. One perfectly normal ten-month-old may be able to walk. His equally normal cousin, born the same week, may not. Neither is "right" or "wrong," "slow" or "fast." Each is growing according to his or her predetermined schedule, and for the parents to force a child to "perform" before he or she is ready may actually stunt his or her development.

Our children's spiritual development takes time, too, as we have already mentioned in our discussion of the wait of faith. It is important here, too, that parents not force growth. Imagine what happens when parents insist on making a child spiritual! They know what good Christians do and don't do and are determined to build these traits into the lives of their children. I assure you, this is futile!

Parents need to remember three important points in this matter of spiritual development:

1. Allow for a spiritual pregnancy in your child's heart before the new birth can take place. It takes time for a developing child to be born. Allow God to germinate His thoughts in your child and bring new spiritual life into the world *in His time*. Parents can cooperate in this process by training a child, that is, offering proper spiritual food in the form of family worship times, Sunday school and church attendance and so on. We will discuss this further in the section on training.

Sincere evangelicals have a tremendous tendency to push their children into decisions for Christ. This is very easy to do with small, vulnerable, eager-to-please youngsters. While a child in a strong Christian home should not be discouraged from spiritual developments, parents need to make sure he is not pushed or manipulated into a profession of faith that is no more than that—a profession. If such "decisions" are made before God's time, they will not represent true salvation and regeneration.

In fact, there is a danger in pushing a child to "pray the sinner's prayer." He or she may be deceived or fooled into thinking he or she has been born again when that may not have happened at all. Many people have been inoculated against genuine Christianity by a false version of it. They may think, "I prayed that prayer, so I must be O.K.," or, "I prayed that prayer and it didn't work for me." Only the touch of the Holy Spirit in His own time and His own way will awaken a child to the gift of eternal life and a personal relationship with Jesus.

2. Parents cannot cooperate with life that isn't there. Before we can expect a child to manifest godly traits he or she needs God's life within. Only God can give this. We can offer training and education, but all of our efforts to develop spiritual life when none is present may bring detrimental results.

Author Eugenia Price once suggested that people who don't know Christ have no reason *not* to swear! The same is true for smaller people—children who have not yet received Jesus as Savior and Lord. Lacking God's life within, they have no reason *not* to manifest worldly actions and attitudes; but these are only symptoms of the root problem: sin.

This does not mean that parents need to tolerate unacceptable behavior in the home. It does mean we shouldn't use God as a club to beat non-Christian children over the head: "It makes God really angry when you do that" or "You know Christians don't act that way!" Such statements merely reinforce a child's feeling that God is a demanding ogre to be avoided at all costs.

If we must object to a particular behavior we need a valid reason: "Smoking is not acceptable in our home because it is an unhealthy habit, and it is discourteous to expose others to unwanted smoke" or "When you swear you offend my Christian beliefs; I am willing to be tolerant and courteous *toward* you, and I expect the same courtesy *from* you, especially when you are living in this house."

3. Once a child becomes a Christian, parents must be ready, in attitude, action and lifestyle, to help him or her cooperate with the new life God has given. Remember: Full maximization of the life of God in any person—in other words, what that life should represent at its fully developed potential—is the stature of the fullness of Christ, His life living in that person.

From birth to the age of thirty Jesus was developing. Then He was able to go out and do a marvelous ministry. One of our weaknesses in the Body of Christ is that we do not allow new Christians time to grow.

Cooperation with a developing Christian's new life will vary, depending on the age at which the person receives the life of God. You cannot treat a seventeen-year-old who has accepted Christ the same as you would treat a seven-year-old who has accepted Christ.

No matter what the age, it is important that you have been a godly parent up to that time so that there will be openness between you and your child and you will be able to help him or her. When children become Christians later in life, any barriers between them and their parents will make their spiritual growth difficult, and will hinder the parents from cooperating with the life of God in their children.

We're ready now to discuss what it means to try to change a child.

Leaving Change to God

Johnnie and I were determined to change the behavior of one of our daughters, particularly the strong will with which she used to pin us to the wall and leave us hanging there! If we told her to go and clean her room, for example, she came up with strong arguments as to why she should not do so, and she continued to argue until she had worn us down. Eventually we would just give up.

Day after day we tried to change her by "picking off the bad fruit," telling her not to argue with us. We insisted she should start behaving "correctly." But the harder we tried, the worse she seemed to get and the deeper the gap between us grew.

Finally we realized that no matter how good our motives were, no matter how sincere we were, we could not change her. Not only was it an impossibility, it was not our God-given responsibility.

Change, or Behavior Modification?

Change, as we use the term here, means a basic and fundamental turnaround in the quality and character of life that results in different behavior patterns.

Now, parents can cause a child to *act* differently, usually by using the threat of punishment or the promise of reward. But there is no fundamental change in the child's character. If there were no form of manipulation, the child would not perform in the desired manner. No change has occurred; the child's behavior has simply been modified.

You have seen this in action. At the circus, for instance, you will see many illustrations of behavior modification. A dog may stand on his hind legs pushing a doll carriage, a monkey dressed in a cowboy outfit may ride horseback, leopards and tigers may leap through flaming circles. These animals are not changed; their behavior has merely been modified. All of them go back to their normal and natural behavior as soon as the show is over.

When we try to change our children spiritually we generally end up producing one of two types of people: hypocrites or rebels.

Hypocrites are playactors, people pretending to be something they are not, acting a certain way without their hearts in it. Hypocrites are joyless people; they cannot be joyful when they have to act in ways inconsistent with their true natures. Pretension causes their religion to be a burden rather than a joy, a set of rules to follow (rules determined, of course, by the group to which they belong). Rules can modify behavior but produce no inner change.

Rebels refuse, either passively (inwardly) or actively (outwardly), to conform to the behavior patterns we are trying to impose upon them. Passive rebellion is much harder to detect in a child than active rebellion.

Both passive and active rebellion are reasons why so many children give up every bit of their religious training the minute they leave home. They go off to work or college and abandon church, God and all religious practices because parents and other well-meaning people have tried to change them.

Behavior modification is not what we are after in rearing our children. But until they are radically changed from within, the best we can hope for is a performance. Until they are new creations in Christ Jesus they may perform for the hope of some reward or the avoidance of some punishment, like hell.

According to a recent article in *Christianity Today* magazine, the number one reason people claim the Christian faith is fear. This is totally inconsistent with the Christian Gospel and completely opposed to God's way of doing things. What has caused this? People have professed the Christian faith without experiencing the transforming change God can make in their lives.

Real Christians are people who are fundamentally changed, and not just trained to act in a certain way. When we are truly changed on the inside, the Christian life is no longer a continual struggle to act in ways inconsistent with our inner being. It is, instead, the spontaneous action of what we are on the inside coming out.

This is what we long for in our children, a change so radical that they do not have to spend the rest of their lives struggling against their natural inclinations.

How does this fundamental change take place in a child's life? It can happen only through Jesus. But we can cooperate with Him in several ways by following these patterns.

1. We need to repent. Repentance is a change of heart that will eventually result in a change of action. Repentance, in one sense, is a gift of God: He shows us where we are wrong. Our part is to agree with Him and accept the truth. When we are able to say, "I am wrong," and not attempt to justify our thinking, then we are ninety percent on the way home to allowing God to change us in the way only He can.

For what do we need to repent? For our failures as Christians and as Christian parents, for our attempts to do what only God can do in drawing our children back to Himself, for our lack of faith in the promises He has given for their eventual redemption.

2. We need to ask God to give our children the gifts of repentance and new life in Him. The Gospel of John tells us that the Holy Spirit comes, in part, to convict the world of sin and of righteousness (16:8–10). We are helpless even to repent without His assistance. We need to ask God to grant our children the conviction of the Holy Spirit that leads to true repentance.

This kind of repentance and change happens within the realm of the spirit, unlike the education we offer in the realm of the soul and body.

To live and minister as Christians and Christian parents we need to understand the difference between the realms of the soul and the spirit.

The soul refers to our personalities and intellects—those traits and characteristics that make us uniquely recognizable individuals. At all levels of life and in all professions or vocations we meet nice, decent, thoughtful, intelligent, well-read but ungodly people. They have characteristics that make them easy to relate to on a human level, and some of those characteristics are even characteristics of God. But those do not make a person a Christian. Any individual can be trained to learn these characteristics to his advantage.

But a Christian is more than just a well-trained human being. He or she has the life of God, which is a gift God gives us through Jesus Christ our Lord. It is a gift we can receive only when the Holy Spirit causes our spirit—that part of us designed to communicate with God—to be open to genuine change, repentance and intimate relationship with Himself. Until God touches each of our children in the spirit they will experience no change.

So our responsibility is not to get them to pray a certain prayer but to pray that they will be touched by God with His life.

3. We need, by the grace of God, to live supernatural lives that will make our children see Jesus in us. Unless we are godly, loving, Spirit-filled, joyous people of faith who demonstrate the life of God consistently in the drudgery and relationships of everyday living, all the talking in the world, all the churchgoing, all the Bible-reading, all the tithing we do will mean nothing to our children. It will be religion, but it will not be Christianity. Joyless, struggle-filled religion will not attract our non-Christian children to our Lord, and it will not draw our wandering children back to Him, either.

The more we rejoice in Him, rather than being negative about any unhappiness in the home, the more successful we will be in the third area of cooperation with God: training.

Training

To train a child means to shape an existing life. It means to educate him or her in all the relational and personal and physical skills he or she will need to get along in the world. Manners, responsibility, pleasant attitudes, morals, the ability to stand up for what is true and honest and right—we are responsible as parents to do our best to instill these in our children, under the guidance and teaching of the Holy Spirit.

God worked hard at training the Israelites, His chosen children. A loving, fair, sometimes stern Father, He gave them the Ten Commandments for successful God-human and human-human interaction. He tried repeatedly to teach them an "attitude of gratitude." He placed enormous responsibility on their shoulders, when He as a Father knew the time was appropriate. And He didn't stop there. He trained His children to know and understand Him and His Law.

We can expose our children to the truth about God and the marvelous stories found in the Bible, and then trust the Holy Spirit to do His work. We do this by means of the family altar, Christian books, music and art in our homes, contact with our own Christian friends from all walks of life, youth outings, exposure to Christian role models, Sunday school and church attendance. (Constant exposure to a dead church, by the way, is one of the worst things we can do to a young person. Parents need to consider moving to a church where the life of God is, no matter how comfortable they are, or in spite of the fact that "we have always been Baptists, or Methodists, or whatever.")

By training our children we accomplish two purposes. One, we give them, early on, when it's easier to learn, the basic skills and abilities they need to get along with others and provide for themselves. The "elementary required courses," so to speak, are then out of the way. Now they can concentrate on learning the refining lessons of the Holy Spirit, which are sufficiently challenging! Young people who come to Christ later in life and have no background in common courtesy, money management and responsible work habits, to name a few, have a huge "course load" to carry all at once. And two, we instill in them the knowledge of God's Word and Christian truths and principles, so that the Holy Spirit can call it to their remembrance (John 14:26) and apply it to their personal needs.

Development, letting God do the changing, and training are three of God's fundamental patterns for parenting. We must understand them in order to cooperate with God in the work of faith. Let's move on, now, to some further parenting tips, or patterns, from our heavenly Father.

9

The Importance of Nurture

In the summer of 1990 I had a "spiritual"—the spiritual counterpart of a physical. For six hours I was examined thoroughly by three godly men in the areas of my soul and spirit.

You might ask, "Why get a spiritual? Did you have some pressing problem that needed to be fixed?" No, but I had a burning desire to be all I can for the glory of Jesus Christ. As a sixty-year-old man I know I am running my last lap on the race course God has laid out for me, and I want it to be the best lap I've ever run. I want to maximize my life. I want to finish well.

I went into my spiritual with two determinations. First, I wanted to answer every question my peers asked as honestly as possible. Second, I wanted to trust the

Lord to reveal any hidden areas that needed to be brought into the open.

A spiritual is not a cure-all. It is a time for insight, a time to deal with the past, set new goals for the future or discover new direction from God to better utilize a person's aptitude and skills.

My spiritual was profitable because all these things happened to some degree. But the major disclosure that came out of it was that as a child I had not been nurtured. I will say more about that later, but first. . . .

What Is Nurture?

Nurturing consists of two basic functions: nourishing and cherishing. Both are essential in rearing children. Both are biblical and, of course, both are qualities God manifests toward us, His children.

Nourishing

To nourish is to feed, and not just with physical food. As people made in the image of God we need nourishment on all three levels of our lives: body, soul and spirit.

The Bible is clear about our responsibility as parents to provide such nourishment for our children, as well. First Timothy 5:8 says, "If anyone does not provide for his own, and especially for those of his household, he has denied the faith, and is worse than an unbeliever." And 1 Thessalonians 2:11 explains how natural it is for a father to provide nourishment for the soul and spirit—"exhorting and encouraging and imploring . . . as a father would his own children."

Few good Christian parents could be accused of failing to provide food, clothing, shelter and health care for their children. Within reason, and within our budgets, we do the best we can to ensure our children's bodily comfort, safety and welfare.

The same cannot be said regarding our children's souls and spirits. Unfortunately, very few homes today offer adequate nourishment in these two areas. Instead, we all too often expect the school, church or outside programs to feed our children.

Scouting programs may do a wonderful job of sharing the importance of patriotism and good citizenship, for example, especially in the cases of children whose backgrounds do not include those values. But a child who sees patriotism manifested in the lives of the two most important people in his life—his parents—is much more likely to grow up loving his country.

In the matter of sex education, parents often neglect totally the need to provide nurture. Many Christian parents fiercely oppose the sex education programs offered by the public schools, but then never give their children any sex education at home. It is no wonder that the statistics for premarital sex and teenage pregnancy among Christian young people are nearly as high as those among secular teens.*

* See *Why Wait?* by Josh McDowell and Dick Day (Here's Life Publishers).

Another soul need: In how many Christian homes do stimulating discussions of current issues take place around the dinner table, offering our young people Christian perspectives on local, domestic and world events? We're more likely to plan the evening's TV watching between mouthfuls!

If we think Sunday school is enough to furnish our children with spiritual food we are in for a great disappointment.

First of all, it was never intended to so do. Sunday school was designed to *supplement* the Christian education given by parents in the home.

Secondly, what is offered in Sunday school is not enough. Most Sunday school teachers are sincere and dedicated, but they are not necessarily good teachers, nor do they always know a whole lot about the subjects they are teaching. And even those who are good teachers and have studied their topics carefully cannot spend enough time with their students to offer much more than information.

Please hear me: I praise God for those Sunday school teachers who give of themselves as role models and nurturers on Sunday morning and beyond! God has certainly used them mightily to affect the lives of children. But no matter how well the good teachers teach and how relevant their material, nothing can take the place of what children see and experience in the home.

The book of Deuteronomy offers a clear directive to parents about this matter of spiritual nurture. Look at chapter 6, verses 5–9:

> "And you shall love the Lord your God with all your heart and with all your soul and with all your might. And these words, which I am commanding you today, shall be on your heart; and you shall teach them diligently to your sons and shall talk of them when you sit in your house and when you walk by the way and when you lie down and when you rise up. And you shall bind them as a sign on your hand and they shall be as frontals on your forehead. And you shall write them on the doorposts of your house and on your gates."

The spiritual nurture of our children is to be a daily, natural part of our lives. Think back on an average week in your home. Did any spiritual nurturing, any natural conversations about the things of God, take place? Once? Twice? Frequently?

It is not my purpose here to give exhaustive instructions about the how-to of spiritual nurture. Many fine books have been written in that field. Take time to visit the family section of your local Christian bookstore to discover the excellent resources available. We need to research the best ways to nurture our children's soul and spirit needs, taking into account their personalities and interests and the schedules and habits of our families. Then we must do it!

Cherishing

To cherish someone is to handle him or her gently and lovingly, especially in the early stages of life when he or she is very weak and tender. All children need to be cherished.

Why? First of all, young children are tender by nature. If you know a child whom you would not call tender, look at his or her environment. The child is probably surrounded by callousness, cruelty, harshness or even just a lack of general good manners and unselfishness. Children normally begin life with very gentle natures.

Secondly, we know that children need to be treated tenderly just by looking at the majority of adults. Most people have been beaten up at some point in their lives and have sore spots. Some are raw all over; some are sore only in certain areas where they have been hurt repeatedly.

Again, the Bible has much to say about cherishing. Isaiah 40:11 is one of many references in which God is pictured as caring gently for us. First Thessalonians 2:7 speaks of the tenderness of a nursing mother for her children, and suggests that Christians need to be equally loving with each other. Ephesians 5:29 mentions the importance of cherishing in the marriage relationship and declares Christ's cherishing love for the Church. Earlier in the same book (4:32) Christians are directed to offer tenderhearted forgiveness and kindness to each other.

Cherishing is a Christian value and practice, yet we have failed miserably. We do not show love and special attention to those who are newborns in body, soul and spirit.

Dudley Hall, a superb minister of God, told me of an astonishing incident that occurred while he was leading a men's retreat in Texas. During one of the sessions he asked the men who had never sat in their fathers' laps and been hugged to come to the front of the room, sit in his lap and allow him to hold them as their fathers should have.

Dudley said the men lined up to do this, and each one who sat in his lap cried his heart out. Here were men who had not been cherished by their fathers.

All forms of life are fragile in their infancy and need special care. We must not deprive our children any longer of their need to be hugged and treated gently and tenderly.

My Own Experience

I mentioned earlier my discovery, in the course of my spiritual, that as a child I had not been nurtured properly. It was a revelation about many of my personality and spiritual lacks, and also about my behavior toward my family.

Several factors contributed to the lack of nurture in my early years. First, since I grew up in a wealthy home in Jamaica in the 1930s, I was partially reared by a nanny, a servant whose chief responsibility was to take care of me. She was a good woman; I remember her pushing me around in a "pram," the British word for a baby carriage.

It was not that my parents did not love me; I know they did. The fact that my primary care was given by an employee in our home was simply part of our culture. Added to this was my mother's insecurity (she was an unwanted child) and her poor health. When I was about two years old she had to leave Jamaica and go by boat to England for surgery. Back in those days it took a long time to make this trip, so my nanny probably gave me more time and care than did any other adult.

Then, at the ripe old age of seven, I went away to a boarding school. (This, too, was a fairly routine practice in the Jamaican upper class.) Run much like a military academy by the teachers and school administrators, the school left the boys to themselves in their dormitories, and you can be sure they did not treat each other with parental gentleness and love. It was more like survival of the fittest.

I was very lonesome for the first month; I remember crying myself to sleep during the opening week. But you don't cry in front of other boys. I had to live with my peers, so after the first four weeks I pretended I didn't care anymore and learned to stop crying. It is hard to imagine now, but after that year I never spent more than three months of any year in my parents' home.

My other school experiences were equally militaristic, with everything run by a bell, life fenced in on every corner and educational techniques intense. Each was a religious school, but I can remember only one teacher and one student who even vaguely resembled what I know now it means to be Christian. This, of course, turned me off to the faith; bad religion in the name of Christ is damaging to one's concept of Christianity.

The point I am trying to make is that in my early childhood my physical and to some extent my soul needs were nourished. But during my school years I received nourishment only in the areas of books and manners. And the tender loving care from being cherished was an unknown quantity.

As I look back on my own parenting years I realize that, in turn, I did not properly nurture my children. I did provide enough nourishment, both physical and spiritual, but I was not tender. I did not know how to cherish. I was never told the need for it and so did not do it.

To my upbringing was added the matter of living up to the image of a macho American man—an idea full of nonsense. We need to rid ourselves of it. It comes nowhere near to the image of God, in all His tenderness, gentleness, firmness, fairness, forgiveness, holiness, lovingkindness and wisdom.

So many times I was rough and hard with my children. I can remember spanking John too harshly. I did not empathize with him or ask his forgiveness. Many times when I said the right things I said them in the wrong way. There was no tenderness in what I said, no kindness, only harshness, contempt and anger.

By the grace of God I have realized, admitted to and sought forgiveness for failing, particularly, to cherish my children. Now I am seeking to make amends for it. Just before I wrote these words I called one of my daughters to see how she was doing since she and her husband are going through a rough time vocationally. In the past I would not have done this, thinking a phone call in the middle of the day a waste of good money. Now that I know the importance of cherishing, I see it as an investment in the nurture of my children's souls and spirits.

Oh, how much we fathers have to learn about fatherhood! And we who are Christians can learn so much from our heavenly Father, if we will, as well as from God-inspired books and from other fathers. We don't know much about golf or woodworking or other such subjects until we study them. We talk about them with other men, read, practice and become knowledgeable. We can do the same with fathering.

Mothers, you see, bond with their children before birth to some extent because they carry them in their wombs for nine months. But other than the act of conception fathers have little to do with their children until they come into the world. So fathers need to make special efforts in the whole area of nurturing. What a difference we could make in our families, our churches and our world if we took seriously this vastly important role!

My childhood in a rich Jamaican home was strongly influenced by Jamaican upper-class culture, just as my children's childhoods were influenced by Southern American culture, and yours are influenced by the culture that predominates where you live. We must remember that because something is culturally acceptable does not mean it is necessarily the best or necessarily Christian. We need to see the difference.

It would be easy to look at my upbringing and say, "That poor neglected child! Nobody cared about him! What kind of society does that to its children?"

Yet we have only to look around us to see that there are millions of children in America today who are not receiving nourishment or cherishing either. In many cases both parents work outside the home in order to uphold a certain standard of living and come home too tired and concerned about household chores to make any investment in the children, except to order them around.

Low-income couples and single parents are under a double burden in this regard. They need to work, sometimes even at two or three jobs, they cannot hire help for household repairs and they are exhausted when their children need special attention.

Other single- or double-income couples may spend plenty of time at home, but are so busy with their hobbies and clubs and friends that the children still lack the nurture they need and might be better off in a good daycare center!

We do not have to do anything God disapproves of, even if it is culturally acceptable. We need the Holy Spirit's direction and discernment as we examine our hearts and lifestyles to make sure our families are taking their proper place on our list of priorities. That proper place is *after* our relationship with God, but *before* ministry opportunities, work, friends and recreation.

Nurturing—nourishing and cherishing—is part of godly parenting, part of cooperating with God as He deals with our children in the work of faith. Our nurturing Father God is our model, our teacher in this important task.

In the next three chapters we will look at ways in which we can use—and control—our tongues to nurture our children's souls and spirits.

10

Mastering the Indicative Mood, or Establishing Relationships God's Way

For a few years I have discipled a group of single men ranging in age from 25 to 35 years. Several months ago I asked them a series of questions about their fathers, including:

- Did your father love you?
- Can you describe your father in one sentence?
- How do you view your father?

Only one of these men was absolutely sure his father loved him. The others *did not know*. Their fathers had not communicated their love clearly—the most important and vital truth in the relationship between father and son.

I made the same mistake with my own children. I communicated plenty of imperatives, or commands, and not nearly enough indicatives, or statements.

To understand this important principle for establishing successful relationships with our children, we need to turn briefly to the Greek language. The New Testament was written in Greek and its usage of Greek verbs offers a vital key to modern-day disciples. Bear with me for a brief explanation, and then we'll apply it to dealing with our children.

A verb is the part of a sentence that affirms action or state of being. This is done in the Greek through voice, tense and mood.

The mood, with which we are interested here, takes either the indicative or imperative form. It defines the action's relationship to reality.

The indicative mood denotes fact or possibility. To say, "He ate" states the fact. To say, "If he eats" states the possibility that he will. Dana and Mantley's *A Manual of Greek New Testament* defines the indicative this way: "The indicative is . . . the mood of certainty. . . . [It] states a thing as true." If I say, "I am a man, sixty years old. I live on Keiser Court and Johnnie is my wife," I am using the indicative mood. These are simple factual statements.

The imperative mood, on the other hand, is used to give a command. When a parent says, "Pick up your clothes," "Clean the garage" or "Take out the garbage," he or she is using the imperative mood. The parent is expressing his or her will, addressing the child's will and expecting a response.

In rearing children parents have to use the imperative mood frequently. It is impossible to do the task of parenting without giving orders and prohibitions:

> "Stop hitting your sister."
> "Brush your teeth every morning."
> "You may not smoke in the house."

Remember: When a parent uses the imperative mood, his or her will is expressed, and the child must decide whether or not to obey. In essence, the use of the imperative sets up a potential confrontation. The indicative mood does not depend on anything the child does. It is simply a statement of fact.

The Way God Did It

A few years ago someone said to me, "Did you know that in the first eight chapters of Romans there is only one verb in the imperative (command) mood?"

I had to admit I did not. Curious, I decided to count the number of times the indicative mood is used in those same eight chapters. To my surprise I found 295 indicative mood verbs. One command to 295 statements of fact! And in the book of Ephesians there are 1101 indicatives as compared with 37 imperatives.

Now here is where an understanding of the Greek moods is important because we gain a new, key truth about God's parenting style. God, in His Word, written by men under the inspiration of the Holy Spirit, wanted to establish certain definite facts *before* He issued commands.

Do you know why?

Read carefully, because when you understand this concept it will enable you not only to live the Christian life in a fuller way, but also to be a better parent as you establish meaningful relationships with your children.

God, our Father, wishes to establish His relationship with each of us based on certain unquestionable realities.

You see, before God tells us to *do* anything He desires that we *know* some things for certain—things that establish His relationship with us, our relationship with Him, the resources available to us and many more certainties. By naming just a few of the 29 indicatives, absolute facts, to be found in Romans 5, for instance, we learn that:

- we have peace with God;
- we have access by faith into this grace;
- we exult in the hope of the glory of God;
- the love of God has been poured out into our hearts;
- we shall be saved from the wrath of God through Christ;
- grace abounds.

These certainties do not depend upon our doing anything, but only on God's grace extended to us in Jesus.

For any relationship to be happy and meaningful both parties must understand what the relationship is (Father God to son or daughter, human parent to human child, employer to employee) and feel assured of the relationship's strength and permanence. Then, and only then, can one party accept commands from the other, because he or she feels secure in the relationship and in the reason for those commands.

I had not seen the Christian life in this light before—as first of all an *absolutely secure relationship*, one of a loving Father committed to me. I had seen it rather as a Master-servant relationship, with the Master (God) giving commands and the servant (me) taking orders. But a relationship built and maintained on performance is never secure and satisfying because both parties know that performances may not always meet expectations.

Here we see the fundamental difference between imperatives and indicatives—a difference with deep implications for parenting. It is the difference between law and love.

Law works primarily in the imperative mood. It says you earn the indicatives—the positive statements—by obeying the imperatives—the commands. "Be a good boy or girl [imperative] so God [or Mommy or Daddy] will love you [indicative]."

Love works primarily in the indicative mood. It says, "Know these things for certain, and then it will be easy to obey: God loves you now, just as you are [indicative]; therefore do good [imperative] as a means of expressing your love back to Him."

If the imperatives (commands) are not *preceded* and *exceeded* by positive indicatives (statements of fact) they will produce adverse reactions in our children—reactions ranging from dislike to insecurity to doubt about the relationship to outright rebellion.

Most parents would be surprised if at the end of a day they could see the number of commands they have issued as compared with the number of assurances. In many cases our use of the imperative far outweighs our use of the indicative.

It is essential to establish certain indicatives with our children before we give them imperatives. And we must continually reinforce and strengthen the indicatives.

Under ideal conditions this should be a fairly easy task. Parents have many opportunities to give small children indicatives before they must begin giving imperatives.

"What a special girl you are!" "Mommy and Daddy are so happy to have you in our family!" "We think you're great!" Sincere, positive actions and words of love and commitment can help a child establish a secure basis from which he or she can receive commands and know they are given in love for the child's own good, and not out of harshness or demand.

Marriage and parenting are about the only major, complicated relational tasks a person can attempt in this life without knowing anything about them! Almost anyone can get a marriage license for a few dollars; no special knowledge is required. And a person can have children and know absolutely nothing about being a parent.

Because we blunder into these complicated relationships and learn the ropes as we go, many of us do not realize we have done a bad or inadequate job of parenting until the children become teenagers. By then many dynamics have been set in motion, and we discover we cannot order our children around in the same way we could when they were small. Having made many mistakes both of omission and commission, we have to develop a different strategy. Unfortunately too many parenting books and seminars offer push-these-buttons-and-you-can-have-wonderful-children formulas, and only involve more imperatives.

It's Never Too Late to Start!

Our children need to know we love them just because we love them, and what this love means in practical terms. And the good news about establishing relationships God's way is that it's never too late to start! You can do it even if your child is in outright rebellion. I am doing it now with my grown children by affirming their worth in my eyes and building them up, indicatives I should have established long ago.

How do we do it? Indicatives need to be established and maintained. We do this in two ways.

First, we employ *verbal repetition*. Just as the Scriptures repeat certain facts about God over and over again, so we need to repeat truths about our relationships with our children frequently. They need to hear us affirm:

1) our unconditional love for them (I will love you regardless);

2) our unqualified acceptance (you are mine and I am yours, period);

3) our reliability and availability (I will be there when you need me);

4) their importance in God's eyes and ours (you were created for a purpose);

5) their worth as individuals (you are unique);

6) their competence and adequacy (I know you can do it!).

This repetition is a never-ending process, but so is the parent-child relationship. And once the indicatives are established in our children's lives they are easier to maintain.

Second, we act in ways that support the truths we have been declaring. Telling a child "I love you regardless" and then screaming because he or she bats a home run through the living room window doesn't strengthen a relationship. Promising to "be there" for a child and then consistently placing other activities (however noble) before family times undermines our credibility.

It is tremendously important to communicate to our children our unconditional love, acceptance and support, as well as vital truths about their worth and adequacy. Then when we give imperatives (as we will have to), our children can receive them on the basis of a healthy, secure relationship.

Our heavenly Father has established indicatives for

us and given us a marvelous pattern for relating to our children. But He has taught and demonstrated another principle as well: He is our *listening* Father. We will discuss His example and how we can model it for our children in the next chapter.

11

The Listening Parent

If your son experimented with drugs last week, would he sit down and share his experience with you? If not, why not? If so, what response would you give him?

If your daughter had a sexual encounter last week, would she feel free to talk with you about it? If not, why not? If so, how would you respond or react?

At the close of our first Sunday morning worship service on January 20, 1991, I received a revelation from God that drastically changed both my conception of Him as my Father and my understanding of what it means to be a listening, accepting, godly parent. It happened this way.

After preaching on our Father's desire for our worship to be in spirit and in truth (John 4:24), I suggested that He wants us to tell Him the way we feel about Him and about what He has done, is doing or is not doing in our lives. I urged the congregation to tell God any "beefs" they had with Him, knowing He would hear them not out of condemnation or judgment, but out of His love. Then they were to listen for His response.

Whatever I ask the congregation to do, I always do myself. So I began to talk to God, telling Him that for a long time I had observed a lack of action on His part with regard to something I considered to be a reasonable request.

I heard Him speak to my heart and say that He was not upset by what I had expressed. In fact, He seemed glad I was being transparent about my feelings, and He wanted me to listen to His explanation of the situation.

I agreed.

Then He said how glad He was I had shared my heart with Him because my honesty allowed Him to teach me in a new area. He was sorry I had not discovered this before, as it would have solved many of my problems.

The teaching was this: My perception of Him as a Father who would not allow me to express my true feelings was living itself out in the type of father I had become to my own children. Not only had I not encouraged them to share their feelings, I had actually *discouraged* them by responding with disappointment, disgust, blame and censure when they did. This was especially true when they had tried to share their feelings of frustration or anger with me as a parent.

As small children, then, our sons and daughters

quickly learned what to share and what not to share with me. But their feelings, though throttled and stuffed deep inside, did not go away. These became the breeding ground for anger, bitterness, resentment, low self-esteem and rebellion.

Not only had I left the children with bad feelings toward me, but I had lost the opportunity to help them know how to handle feelings.

Thoughts tumbled through my head quickly. Where had my misconception of my heavenly Father come from?

While I believe we are all responsible for our own actions, we do model our behavior and thinking on our background and upbringing. I do not wish to place blame on my parents, but two factors from my childhood undoubtedly accentuated my lack of good listening skills. Perhaps these will sound familiar to you, or will help you identify some other factors in your background that affect the way you listen to and communicate with your children.

First, I remembered the philosophy of most of my parents' adult friends, one that was common for that generation: "Children should be seen and not heard." In fact, I can recall clearly being patted on the head while some adult on the tennis court repeated this saying.

Second, since religion in our home was of a very legalistic nature, especially as expressed by my mother, I would never have thought of sharing my feelings about certain failures. The way I heard the adults in my home talk about those who drank or committed adultery was absolute insurance I would not admit to such sins if I did commit them!

For the first time in my life, that morning in January, I saw clearly that our God of truth wants me to share the truth of what is going on inside of me. Then I can listen for His explanation, response and help. This was an awesome revelation. It was as if a 500-watt lightbulb had been turned on inside my head. I began to see what kind of heavenly Father we have, and what kind of ungodly father I had been. I repented!

There is an amazing verse in the Psalms that underscores the idea of truthfulness in our relationship with God. It is Psalm 137:9: "How blessed will be the one who seizes and dashes your little ones against the rock." And that is the end of the chapter. No explanation comes after it.

What in the world are we to gather from such a quotation?

Let me tell you the context in which we find this verse. Psalm 137 is the expression of a Jewish captive in Babylon. One of his captors had tauntingly asked him to sing a song of Zion, his homeland. Not surprisingly, the captive not only had lost his song, but was feeling bitter and resentful. Out of these emotions came his angry thoughts toward his captors: "I wish someone would take your children and throw them against the rocks!"

Why did God allow these words to be recorded in the holy Scriptures? *Because He wants us to know it is all right to tell Him how we are feeling.* He will never reject or condemn us for sharing what is in our hearts. When we tell Him our feelings, He is able to help us work through them.

We read in the New Testament that we are to "come boldly unto the throne of grace, that we may obtain mercy, and find grace to help in time of need" (Hebrews 4:16, KJV). This is God's invitation to those of us who have "blown it," who have sinned and behaved badly. We can get all the help we need to repent of and recover from the things we have done.

What a gracious God we serve! Oh, that I had been this kind of father to my own children!

Breaking the Cycle

The destructive cycle of stifling people, not allowing them to express their thoughts and feelings, must be broken somewhere. I am seeking to do it in my family line, and I pray God will help me be successful.

The Monday morning after God spoke to me so clearly about the importance of being a listening parent, I wrote a letter to my children, repenting for this failure and asking their forgiveness. After describing my revelation from God, I continued with these thoughts:

> I realize I have not given you the same freedom [God] has given us all. It has become clear to me that my responses to you have more often made it easier for you not to share with me what you were really feeling. I realize that I put you down, I condemned you. . . . Much of this came out of wrong thinking

and attitudes on my part—my impatience, my gruffness and hard way of speaking, my lack of understanding that you were children and were acting like children, my strong convictions and wrong ideas about parent-child relationships . . . the "children should be seen and not heard" philosophy of my childhood. [All these] kept me from being the kind of father I could have and should have been.

For this I repent and ask your forgiveness. I ask you to share with me anything and everything that might be in your heart out of the past—no matter what—so we can have clear communication and thus communion and a deeper love. I understand you might have some very unpleasant things to share and say—I am prepared for this and accept it as part of the price I must pay for my failure to be a godly father.

Thank God the "ballgame is not over." I desire to finish well, to be the best for you and for God. In the future please feel free to express to me anything and everything you feel or think. I will listen and respond by the grace of God as I should. This does not mean I will agree, but I will listen and respect your point of view. . . .

In all probability I will fail at times. When I do, please remind me of this letter. Pray I will make all the inner adjustments that will make me the kind of father God is.

I urge you in the light of all this to do two things. First, always tell your Father God how you think and feel. Hide nothing. Be totally open to Him. He will hear with sympathy and understanding. Then listen to Him, give Him a chance to respond to You. Yield in faith and trust to Him . . . remembering it is really

> impossible for a child to understand all a father does or says.
>
> Second, pray you can create an atmosphere with your children that will enable them to tell you everything, failures as well as successes. In this way you can be God's full agent to them.
>
> I have shared my heart . . . and ask forgiveness. God is good and I am sure you will be. Whatever there is between us let's get rid of it for His sake and for ours and our children's.

The children have responded to me since then. My two sons were able to express in a good way how they felt in their hearts. At my request, one of them gave me a list of the things I had failed in from his point of view.

One daughter, the child most like me, explained she had already told me in the past how she felt, and she had, when we had some very hurtful arguments.

I am grateful to God that at this point in our lives our relationships are good and getting better.

Perhaps the hypothetical situations I described at the beginning of this chapter were more real in your life than not. Perhaps your children used to come to you and talk, but don't anymore. A parent's reactions to a child's failures at an early age set the pattern for communication in the later years.

I hope that this chapter has encouraged you as we have talked about the tremendous listening parent we have in our Father God. Knowing what He is like and that through the indwelling Holy Spirit He can give us the power to be like Him should steer us away from guilt over our past failures with our children.

First John 1:9 says that if we confess our sins, He is faithful and just to forgive us our sins, and to cleanse us from all unrighteousness. What a loving heavenly Father we have! And how He longs for us to share His kind of listening, fatherly love with our children.

12

Giving Glory

One of the greatest errors of my life in dealing with people in general and with my children in particular has been my failure to give them glory, the glory due them as individuals created by God with unique talents, abilities and personalities. One result was that at least one of my children hung around with "the wrong crowd" because those people gave him glory: They appreciated him verbally and non-verbally when I had failed to do so.

The need for glory—another way of describing self-worth, significance or value in one's own eyes—is a soul need. Even as the human body has certain needs and desires that must be met for growth and health, so the soul, the real inner person, has basic cravings that must be fed.

We are aware of physical needs but not quite as conscious of our soul needs. The mother who would never think of letting her baby go unfed in body may well be starving the same child's soul.

It is important for parents to realize that God has designed a healthy and proper way to meet every legitimate need an individual has. If that need is not met in the right, God-ordained way, the individual will be driven to seek fulfillment somewhere else.

Have you ever seen a person eating out of a garbage can and been revolted? How in the world could he or she do that? Remember: A starving person will eat *anything*. The devil knows how to use our driving needs to our destruction, tempting us to satisfy our needs in God-forbidden ways. Starving souls are easy prey and targets for the enemy.

The dictionary defines glory as exalted praise, honor or distinction bestowed by common consent. Glory makes a person feel honored, illustrious or significant.

As I mentioned earlier, glory is another word for self-worth or self-love. And we all need proper self-worth as food for the soul. After all, we live with ourselves; if we do not like ourselves we are in trouble, for we have no way to escape. But if we really love ourselves as Jesus commanded us to do (Mark 12:31), we are secure enough to love other people and deal fairly and kindly even with those who dislike us.

You see, the Christian life is walked out on two "legs": one is a proper self-image and the other is a proper image of God, knowing God as He really is, not as the caricature we so often see of Him. Each is basic and essential to satisfactory, and satisfying, Christian living.

The vast majority of Christians I know have at least one severely damaged leg, if not two. If either leg is faulty, a Christian will limp through life, despite all other advantages or privileges.

One of our parental responsibilities, which we have already discussed, is to educate our children properly in the things of God, giving them accurate pictures of who He is. But we also need to impart the truth about ourselves as children of God—that we were created in His image, are of vast worth in His sight and, no matter what we have done, can be restored to a full and intimate relationship with Him.

I want to make one important distinction here: There is a difference between a *damaged* self-image and an *immature* one. An immature understanding of oneself is natural, and is matured through the processes of life. Proper care of any living thing will result in proper growth. A damaged self-image must be healed and restored.

Two Types of Damaged Self-Images

A person manifests a damaged self-image in one of two ways: by thinking too much of himself or by thinking too little of himself.

Those who think too much of themselves are called

"proud," and pride is an abomination to God. He knows, of course, when pride is caused by a damaged self-image. He longs to work with us to heal it and remove the false partitions that block our hunger for His righteousness.

Many Christians have interpreted the fact that they think too little of themselves as humility. It is not: It is inverted pride. A person with this problem seeks to call attention to himself or herself because of perceived deficiencies. While inverted pride is not as objectionable to others as is thinking too much of oneself, it is just as damaging, and makes a wholesome life impossible.

From my experience I would say that there are at least twenty people who think too little of themselves for every one who thinks too much of himself. The Scriptures teach us to strive for balance in our self-images: "I say to every man among you not to think more highly of himself than he ought to think; but to think so as to have sound judgment, as God has allotted to each a measure of faith" (Romans 12:3). Or, as the Phillips translation puts it, "Don't cherish exaggerated ideas of yourself or your importance, but try to have *a sane estimate of your capabilities* by the light of the faith that God has given to you all" (italics mine).

God's Design for Healthy Self-Images

Parents: God's design for the nurture and growth of healthy self-images in our children involves us! We are to be the source from which our children fill their inner soul needs for glory, value, self-worth. If children do not get glory from us, they will get it somewhere else.

Why do I say this is God's design? Because Jesus, God's own Son, received His glory from His Father. "It is My Father who glorifies Me," Jesus told a group of people on one occasion (see John 16:14). And we all remember the Father saying from heaven, "This is My beloved Son, in whom I am well-pleased" (Matthew 3:17). What His Father thought of Him was what Jesus prized most.

Just so, the glory our children receive from us seems to matter more to them than any other glory, even if they won't admit it. That is why self-images damaged in the home by neglect and ignorant parenting are so difficult to heal. When tender life forms are hurt by the grower, the damage is painful. One angry young adult woman, whose father had sexually molested her and whose mother had rejected her, still slept with her teddy bear—a gift from parents who never gave her the glory she so desperately needed.

We give glory to our children in at least three ways: by the spoken word, by rewards and by increased responsibilities.

Words, Words, Words

In the entire realm of spiritual health nothing is more important than words. What money is to commerce, words are to the inner person. Words are literally soul food.

Parents, then, can most easily and often feed their children's soul needs for glory with words—words of praise, affirmation, commendation, approval and applause. Watch a small child's face light up when his mom or dad exclaims over a picture or school paper he has done. Watch a child of any age brighten when a parent expresses approval of an attitude or action. And fathers, watch your teenage daughter's reaction when you compliment her appearance or treat her with gentlemanly courtesy. This kind of glory-giving may do more than you'll ever know to reinforce her in her search for healthy male-female relationships.

Words of affirmation are particularly important. Tell your child you appreciate who he or she *is*: "I like you for yourself, for all the qualities and traits that make you you." Make sure your children receive not only performance-based appreciation, but affirmation of their worth as human beings.

Rewards

Another way of giving glory is by rewards. Dinner out with Dad or Mom, a party in honor of an achievement, a birthday celebration, a new dress, a special privilege, a little extra spending money—all may say, "You've done well." Rewards tend to affirm performance, so be careful to balance them with affirmation for the inner person, as well.

Responsibility

Increasing a child's responsibilities may also give him or her glory. By this I don't mean loading on chores. I mean things like allowing a teenage son to run errands with the family car, to care for a younger brother or sister occasionally or to help out in the family business. This may be a way of saying, "We trust you and believe you are capable of doing this important task."

One family we knew had a lovely daughter, Janie, their youngest child, whose low sense of self-worth finally manifested itself in a suicide attempt. The girl's therapists suggested to her parents that they give Janie some absolutely necessary, vital chore to help her feel indispensable.

Janie's mother told me, "Reflecting on what the therapist said, I remembered that before assigning household chores to the older children we asked each one to tell us which job he or she disliked the most and which one he or she disliked the least. Then each was allowed to choose his or her task and taught how to do it properly. As the children began to receive praise for their specialties the work always, without fail, improved drastically.

"We realized that in raising Janie we had drifted away from this practice. During a family work assignment time we encouraged her to select more difficult work. She picked cleaning the kitchen and became the best ever at it. Her face still lights up when I ask, 'Would you please get the kitchen in shape? When you do it I know it will be perfect.' "

God's Glory and the World's

In this matter of giving glory, just as in any parenting task, we need the guidance and wisdom of the Holy Spirit to help us give His kind of glory, not the world's.

The world's glory is often superficial, insincere and manipulative. It may be overdone or driven by selfishness or ulterior motives. Unless we are giving glory out of the resources of God's love and wisdom, our children will sense that it is false. False glory, the world's glory, will not satisfy our children's soul needs.

Another thing about the world's glory: It can change in a fraction of a second. I remember hearing a runner in one of the Olympic competitions tell how reporters gathered around him when they thought he had won a race. But when the officials announced he had really been beaten by one one-hundredth of a second, the flock left him in an instant to crowd around the newly announced winner.

The world recognizes with glory only those who are better than others, thus enabling only a few persons to receive its praise.

But God's kind of glory is real, lasting and available for all to receive. If we parents are working with God and listening to His directions as we deal with our children we will give glory on His behalf—the right amounts to the right child at the right time. It can be a vital link in the work of faith God is doing in their lives.

13

Money in the Bank

How many times I have been frustrated with my children because they would not receive what I was giving them—good stuff in the way of Christian education or guidance! It was even more frustrating to know that they were eager to receive from their friends advice and information that I knew was detrimental to their spiritual and emotional growth.

Why won't our children listen to us and benefit from what we want to offer them? After all, look at all we have done for them!

The answer, often, is that we do not have "money" in their "banks," and their friends do.

Think of it like this. Suppose I get a notice from my bank that says: "Your account is overdrawn. We have returned your check in the amount of $191.89 to the Alligator Plumbing Company. Your account has been charged an overdraft fee of $20.00."

This would indicate that my transactions in this matter were deficient. And if I choose to make such transactions a regular practice it will not be long before the bank breaks off its relationship with me.

The same is true in our personal relationships. How often have you said, as I have, "After all I've done for that child I don't understand why we don't have a good relationship. Why isn't he or she willing to accept my good advice?"

An honest mental review reveals the truth. You and I may have put much into our children's lives, providing not only the basic necessities but luxuries, too. We may have given them all kinds of things—*except what they wanted or counted as valuable.*

The Laws of Banking

We can understand an important dynamic of developing good relationships by looking at two basic laws of banking.

One, deposits must exceed withdrawals. This is fairly simple: We must put in more money than we take out. It is not enough to keep deposits and withdrawals equal because the bank may keep some of our money for handling our accounts.

Two, deposits must be made in a currency accepted by the bank. An item may be of great value to you or me, yet be totally unacceptable to the bank. A product considered valuable for bartering by the members of a remote tribe in Africa—cows, for example—may not be useful as currency in New York City.

How These Laws Work in Relationships

All relationships, especially those between parents and children, are best established by keeping the proper balance between deposits and withdrawals.

What are deposits? Deposits are anything and everything we do for someone else that has value in his eyes. Deposits communicate, "You are important to me; I care for you. I love you. You count as far as I'm concerned." Topics we have discussed like nourishing and cherishing, using indicatives, listening and giving glory can all be deposits.

The parent-child relationship begins when the parent makes a deposit in the child's life. Parents certainly feel that the acts of giving birth to and nurturing a baby are deposits, though they may be thrown in our faces later: "I never asked to be born!"

While deposits at first may seem to be all on the parent's part, once the child begins to cuddle and smile the relationship is grounded, for no relationship can be established or maintained by one person. The more deposits each makes in the other's life, the stronger the relationship.

I once asked one hundred men to tell me the most memorable thing they had ever done with their fathers. The number one answer was "The time we went fishing together." Another top one was "The time I went to work with Dad." Few other events even registered. Fishing together and going to work together counted as deposits for those boys. They were activities that really communicated fatherly love and concern.

What are withdrawals? Imperatives—commands—will count as withdrawals. In our home we expected everyone to participate in the household duties necessary to maintaining our life together as a family: "Ruth Ann, please wash the dishes; John, please mow the lawn."

Other requests for help, which are a necessity in the give and take of all relationships, are usually withdrawals, too. This is especially true when the requests all come from the parent or all come from the child, making for a one-sided relationship. If properly balanced, however, our requests for help can make the other party feel needed and appreciated, thus giving glory—a deposit.

Negative encounters that put strain on our parent-child relationships are also withdrawals. When John and I had an argument over his failure to wash the car one day, as he had promised he would, I lost my temper with him and strained our relationship. I once promised Ruth Ann I would take her shopping but had to renege because of a last-minute church meeting. As she was disappointed, my broken promise was a withdrawal.

Just as a bank account can stand only so many withdrawals, so it is with our parent-child relationships. We need to make sure there have been enough deposits to cover them.

Jim was a freshman in college when he came to live in

our home, and ever since then we have considered him one of our family, a precious son. He had been on his own ever since his parents died, and told us he needed and wanted a family, especially the input of a godly man in his life.

Being part of a family seemed to give Jimmy real joy. It was a deposit, as far as he was concerned. But was it enough to counteract the withdrawals we were making, particularly when I disagreed with this independent young man's decisions on occasion, and asked him to consider my advice?

Johnnie has shared with me that one morning Jim came into the room where she was having her quiet time. He was beginning to wonder if he had made the right choice in moving in with us. He had not realized, he said, that having the input of a godly man in his life might mean some of his opinions and decisions would be up for discussion!

Asking the Lord to give her wisdom and guide her words, Johnnie reassured Jimmy that I would always advise him out of a caring heart, even if he sometimes misunderstood me.

Years later Jimmy wrote me that he knew we loved him when we advised him, at one point, not to quit college to go on the road for a year with a Christian singing group. Apparently the deposits the Lord helped us to make in Jim's life did exceed the withdrawals!

Back to Basics

Here we return to the basic building blocks for this book: Christian parents need to be relating intimately to

God and cooperating with Him if they want to know which deposits and withdrawals are acceptable in the life of each individual child. This matter of deposits and withdrawals may become glaringly evident when a child leaves God. At a time like that, we parents are often made uncomfortably aware—sometimes by the wandering child—that we have taken out too much.

Here are three general principles to keep in mind as you seek God's guidance about making deposits in the lives of your children.

1. Give of yourself. Giving of yourself is vital and always means giving quality time—quality time, that is, as considered acceptable by the child.

In trying to express love to John once when he was quite young, I promised to take him to Disney World. Personally I have an intense dislike for that kind of amusement; I get bored. So, seeking to fulfill this obligation and still please myself, I decided to get another dad to come and take his child so the two children could play on the rides together while the fathers kept each other company.

I ended up calling several persons. Each one, in turn, agreed to go but then called back to say something had come up.

One day as I was thinking about the situation I said out loud, "I wonder what the Lord is trying to say to me?" Immediately Ruth Ann, who was in the same room, answered, "Maybe He is telling you to go and have a good time with John yourself."

Either I never heard her, or I turned her comment off because it did not meet my need. The trip fell through; we didn't go at that time because I had set conditions on it, conditions for meeting *my* need, not John's.

One day some time later when I was questioning the Lord about this, He said quite clearly, *I spoke to you through Ruth Ann. I wanted you to go alone with John, because that is what he needs.*

Wow! I never thought God would speak to me through a teenager. What a mistake! I sought immediately to remedy the situation. John and I went to Disney World by ourselves, and I learned a lesson: I was more interested in my happiness than in giving of myself to John, and that attitude could not put money in his bank.

2. Give gifts and activities of genuine interest to the child and not just you. This will differ with children's sexes, ages and interests. Jimmy and I may listen to some music he has written. If I go to a movie with John it should be one of his choice. If Ruth Ann wants to play checkers I shouldn't insist we play gin rummy.

You may want to introduce your child to the classics by reading *Treasure Island* together, but if that is not his or her idea of a good time, he or she will consider it a withdrawal. I'm not saying parents can't carry out such activities; just be sure that they are balanced with deposits that the *children* consider deposits. Many times in our relationships with our children Johnnie and I thought we were doing things they would be happy about, only to discover later we had made unacceptable deposits; they had not registered or been received. And some of the deposits they would have received, we did not give.

3. When you see a need in your child's life, make a deposit. Here again we must pay attention to the most fundamental principle of all: walking in the Spirit according to His wisdom and directions. He alone can help us connect certain behaviors as our children's ways of expressing their needs. And He can help us know what deposits will fill those needs.

"Mommy, I don't feel like going to school today."

Johnnie told me she had noticed that Ruthie was beginning to say this quite often. Finding nothing wrong physically, she would send an unhappy little girl off to school, much to her own motherly distress.

So Johnnie went to our heavenly Father for His understanding of the situation. He prompted her to reflect on what day, in particular, Ruthie was feeling "sick." Sure enough, Johnnie realized it was always on Tuesday. The next Tuesday morning, when Ruthie began to complain of feeling ill, Johnnie asked, "Ruthie, what do you do at school on Tuesdays?" Ruthie broke into tears.

"Oh, Mommy, we have art today. I can't stand it! It makes me sick to my stomach. Mine is always the worst in the class. Everybody else loves art."

Johnnie, who had always hated the creative arts, too, because she felt she was not good at them, related to Ruth Ann's frustration. The Holy Spirit prompted her to offer our daughter the comfort He had offered her earlier in life.

"Ruthie, God created each person with his or her own gifts. These gifts are often different, making each person special because they are not like everyone else. You have a sweet spirit and a love for people. These are wonderful gifts from God! You don't have to be the best in art; just relax and do the best you can. That will make your father and me happy."

Johnnie's loving, empathetic words apparently helped Ruthie. And, thanks to the wisdom and understanding given by our loving Father, she knew how to encourage and pray for our daughter on Tuesdays.

Johnnie had made a deposit—giving glory and indicatives—that filled a need in Ruth Ann's life.

Deposits and withdrawals. Nearly all of the verbal and nonverbal exchanges between parent and child fall into one of these two categories. With God's direction we can learn to balance our children's bank accounts so that their needs will be met.

14

Responding to the Gaps

A gap is the space that exists between what is and what ought to be.

Our world is full of gaps. People are full of gaps. Leaders are full of gaps. Institutions are full of gaps. All of these are easy to see—with the exception, of course, of the gaps in our own lives!

We are affected mostly by gaps in those who are close to us—our spouses, our children, members of our extended families, the neighbors, the people we work with, the other Christians at our church. Gaps in people to whom we relate infrequently are not nearly as troublesome.

When we look at parent-child relationships, we find that the hardest gaps to handle are those between our expectations of each other's behavior, and the actual behavior.

Among other behaviors during his rebellious period, John started chewing tobacco and dipping snuff. I cannot tell you how objectionable this was to me personally, not to mention the idea of John's physical wellbeing and social acceptability.

I saw other gaps in John, as well. Many times he had the wrong kind of friends. His room was untidy. He refused to take his studies seriously.

At the same time, John was seeing gaps in me, his father. I am sure these were as bothersome and annoying to him as his were to me. One time he gave me a list of them, which follows:

> You speak down to me when you are angry . . .
>
> You go from one extreme to another . . .
>
> You give destructive criticism . . .
>
> You say one thing and do another . . .
>
> You do not give me much personal communication . . .
>
> You give me gifts, rather than affection . . .
>
> You hold things over my head in order to keep me under control.

Right or wrong, he perceived me in this way—filled with gaps. To many of them I could only plead "Guilty." But I put them *all* into my prayer book, so I could pray about them.

Parents and children all have gaps in their lives, big ones and small ones, serious ones and insignificant ones, inherited ones and developed ones, injury-inflicted ones and choice ones, real ones and imaginary ones. Living with each other makes us constantly aware of these gaps, and there is nothing wrong with seeing them. In fact, the Lord often shows them to us.

The big question is: When you see a gap in your child—the wrong type of friend, low or failing grades, bad study habits, sloppy or unconventional dress, drug or alcohol use—how do you respond? We have two choices: intercession or accusation.

Intercession and Accusation

Have you ever had someone "go to bat" for you when the solution to your problem was beyond your ability? Do you remember how you felt toward the person who stepped in on your behalf? Did you feel a deep sense of gratitude? A desire to repay him or her in some way? A closeness?

The person who goes to bat for you is called an intercessor, one who intervenes, mediates, interposes on your behalf, sometimes at great cost to himself.

Now think about it from this angle. Do you have any problem remembering how you felt toward people who, in your time of need, responded with blame, censure, condemnation, criticism, fussing or accusation? Are you drawn to such people? Do you want to be around them? Do you want them as friends?

Of course not. Their reactions leave us feeling

- inferior
- unworthy

- inadequate
- hopeless and
- full of self-pity and guilt.

Someone who responds to a need by blaming, condemning, censuring and criticizing is called an accuser.

The Bible calls the devil an accuser, because he delights in reminding us (and God) of our sins and mistakes. By doing so he discourages us, making us feel all of those bad feelings listed above. The devil has a certain future, however: "The accuser of our brethren has been thrown down, who accuses them before our God day and night" (Revelation 12:10).

When God saw the gaps in our behavior, the big spaces that exist between His rightful expectations of us and our willful actions, what did He do? When He looked at the gap that separated us from Him, cutting off intimate fellowship between us, what was His response?

He could have accused, and been perfectly right and just in doing so, but He did not. He made a plan to fill the big gap of our severed relationship with Him, and the resulting gaps caused by our separation.

He sent Christ into our world, not to accuse or condemn us, but to save us by His death on the cross and through His resurrection. Our God provided all that would be necessary to close the gaps between ourselves and Him. And now Jesus sits in heavenly places interceding for us with perfect compassion and understanding.

As Romans 8:34 puts it, "Christ Jesus is He who died,

yes, rather who was raised, who is at the right hand of God, who also intercedes for us." And Hebrews 7:25 says, "He [Jesus] is able to save forever those who draw near to God through Him, since He always lives to make intercession for them."

Jesus can speak on our behalf because He lived on earth in a body like ours. He experienced firsthand the stress that the evil one brings against all people. He knows how difficult it is, and He knows all we go through. He was "in all points tempted like as we are, yet without sin" (Hebrews 4:15, KJV).

When we are in union with Christ Jesus, the gap between God and us is completely filled. We are complete in Him, and as far as God is concerned a gap no longer exists.

We evangelicals need to learn this truth: We have been justified, made righteous, in Jesus—as righteous as Jesus is righteous. We each have a perfect relationship with God.

We can, of course, draw closer to Him in fellowship. But He can never draw closer to us than He already has. Our relationship with Him is made complete in Christ. It is a gift, a privilege, an opportunity.

Now we must take advantage of the fact that God is our Father. If we are truly seeking to pattern our parenting after that of our heavenly Father, and if we are in union with Jesus, we will respond to gaps in our children in the way He would.

Does accusing our children help them change?

Does it give them hope?

Does it encourage them?

Of course not. Accusation discourages and leads to destruction of the fellowship that could exist between us. All of our fussing, accusing and blaming John for his dipping and chewing did not help one little bit. We learned a big lesson from this: He is still our son, regardless of what he does, but he will not hang around us if all we do is criticize. If he does not hang around us, we will have no input in his life. Since he is a social animal, as we all are, he will then run around with the people who do accept him, people who do not care about or criticize him for his faults and gaps.

Accusation only destroys relationships.

Intercession releases God to be God in all the situations of life. For some reason He chose to allow Himself and His actions to be limited by the extent of our prayers.

"You do not have because you do not ask," James reminds us (4:2). Often we do not have those things we desire for others simply because we did not ask God to provide them. When we ask Him, He acts—in His own way and time, but He acts.

Many times I have suddenly become aware that a change has occurred, a gap has been filled in one of our children. Then I realize I shouldn't be surprised: It is what I have been interceding for, asking God for. And often, as I intercede before Him on behalf of one of my children, He instructs me how to cooperate with Him in responding to or filling a gap. This is part of the work of faith.

During his high school years Richard read one book, and that, as best we can remember, was under duress! He was not what you would call a student. We tried not to criticize or make unhelpful remarks about this gap. Instead we interceded, asking God to change Richard so he would be able to handle university courses and learn to love all the riches books can offer.

Amazingly (although not in God's eyes) Richard became a lover of history. To love history, you must be an avid reader. He was changed, and has stayed that way ever since. As he is now a minister, a profession that requires him to do much reading, we are very grateful.

We had much the same experience with John, except the miracle is greater. John ceased any serious study when he was a sophomore in high school. He barely made it through and then in his first year of college was placed on probation. Here was a gap that needed to be filled!

Through intercession, and obedience to the direction of the Holy Spirit for dealing with John, the gap *was* filled: In junior college John made the dean's list!

Remember: God is the Creator, the Changer. He alone can create a new life, a new heart, a new man or woman. Our part is to intercede, releasing God to do in others what He knows needs to be done, and not what we think needs to be done.

Whatever we are, we are because of the intercession of Christ and of others in His Body. Whatever our children are, they are because of the intercession of Christ, ourselves and others who care deeply enough to pray for them. If this is not true, what would be the point of prayer?

Mistakes We Make in Gap-Filling

It is easy for us as sincere, earnest Christian parents who want the best for our children to jump in without the Holy Spirit's leading, and thus make mistakes. Here are three mistakes we make often.

1. We seek to fill gaps that are filled only by the maturing process. Many behaviors we perceive as gaps in our children are due to immaturity—literally, to childishness. Some changes will simply come in the natural course of the God-ordained maturing process. Perhaps you have heard parents criticize a small child for refusing to sit still through a long, late evening church service. How unfair! Small children need many hours of sleep, and to accuse them of naughtiness when they are simply too tired to cooperate is to misunderstand normal patterns of child development.

Through intercession, intimate relationship with our heavenly Father and openness to resources He brings along (books, speakers and so on) we can find out how to cooperate with Him to provide an environment where children can mature emotionally, mentally and spiritually, as well as physically.

2. We have unrealistic expectations of performance. I often got angry at John because he was not enthusiastic about yard work early on Saturday mornings. I thought this showed a gap of laziness and indifference. I was determined to fill that gap—not only to make him perform, but to make him perform with the right attitude, as well!

You can guess how much success I had. It was unrealistic for me to expect a teenager to *want* to cut lawns on Saturday morning. This is not to say I was wrong in giving him chores and responsibilities; I simply needed to make sure my expectations took his age and humanity into account.

3. We seek to fill the spiritual gap. We have mentioned already this passion on the part of Christian parents to get our children to make decisions for Christ as quickly as possible. Much of our motivation is out of fear, which can be alleviated by getting a word of faith for our wandering children, and then acting on it in the walk and work of faith.

Yes, children can and do accept Christ at early ages, but let's let God do it in His time and way. Manley Beasly, a choice servant of Christ who is now with his Lord, used to tell me he did not go by what his children said about their relationships with God. He looked, instead, for changed lives. This is scriptural.

If we push children too far and too fast in filling spiritual gaps they will react in one of two negative ways. First, they may rebel, outwardly or inwardly. Outward rebellion may manifest itself as stubbornness, hostility and disobedience. Inward rebellion, far more subtle and terribly dangerous, causes children to conform because it is expedient to do so. But as soon as they leave home they drop out of everything spiritual.

Second, children who are pushed into early "decisions" for Christ can become little Pharisees. In my opinion this is worse than rebellion. These children know and say all the right words and do all the right things. But their hearts are not changed. The Christian Church is full of such people, plastic Christians performing evangelical rituals. Rituals are not wrong if they come out of a changed heart. But without changed hearts to motivate them, such performances are spiritually empty and dead.

How to Respond

Yes, our children have gaps, many of them. Some may never go away. How should Christian parents respond?

1. Stay in union with Christ. This will help you become an intercessor. See accusation as none of your business. When you do fall into accusation, confess it as sin before God and ask your children to forgive you. Having to ask anyone for forgiveness is strong motivation for not doing something again!

2. Seek His voice. As you intercede before God for your children, ask Him how you can cooperate with Him in the work of faith.

3. Remember that many gaps are perceived gaps. Some gaps are due only to the culture or the age or gifting of your child. They may also be projections of your own gaps. Ask God to give you discernment about this.

Intercession, not accusation, is God's way of responding to gaps. In the next chapter we will explore some principles God has taught Johnnie and me as we have interceded for our children's gaps. They involve cooperating with Him in drawing the lines that govern our children's behavior.

15

Knowing Where to Draw the Lines

"Take that damn earring off, or get out of this house," exploded Gene, a deacon and dedicated member of my church, when he saw an earring dangling from his son's ear.

Sitting in my office relating this story, Gene looked at me with a sheepish smile and continued, "As soon as those words came out of my mouth the Holy Spirit said, *What about your tattoo?*

"I remember clearly the day I came home from the Army and walked into the kitchen, peeling off my shirt," Gene explained. "The moment my mother saw the dagger I'd had tattooed on my arm, she burst into tears. My father, hearing her sobs, rushed in to investigate. He saw the tattoo, understood her tears and blurted out, 'I wonder what in hell he'll do next!' "

"Gene," I said, as we both broke into loud laughter, "I think it's wonderful you've grown so much as a Christian that right in the middle of all that emotional conflict and anger you heard God speaking so clearly!"

To Fight or Not to Fight

Why was Gene asking for my help and advice about his son's behavior? Because he knew I had gone through an "earring crisis" myself. Such concerns about cultural conformity, behavior and apparel seem to consume lots of parental energy and attention, especially during our children's adolescent stages.

John was about eighteen when he told us he was going to get his ear pierced. I reacted just as Gene did, except I do not think I said *damn* out loud. But I did put my foot down. No son of mine would be caught dead wearing an earring!

Since we were already having trouble with John on many other fronts, this just intensified the battle. One of our other children, who had observed several of our verbal skirmishes, called me and said, "Dad, don't draw the line here. This isn't a serious matter, and it's not worth fighting over."

Usually I am not a very good listener, especially during emotional stress. But this time I was. After thinking (and, I believe, praying) it over, I yielded reluctantly to the good advice and stopped objecting to John's getting his ear pierced.

Two incidents that happened within a short period of time cured me not only of "anti-earringism," but of a lot of other personal "anti's," and gave me much-needed insight from the Holy Spirit in this matter of drawing lines and determining acceptable boundaries for our children's behavior.

Incident Number 1. Mike was a young man in our church who wore an earring and had long hair. To call him unconventional would be to put it mildly. Yet he was the only young man in our church who really reached out to John in a consistent way, a way John would accept, when he was in the worst stages of rebellion. Here in our church, mostly full of "straights," one of the few "non-straights" reached out effectively to John. How could I feel judgmental toward him?

Incident Number 2. After John's initial turnaround toward a relationship with Jesus he headed off to college. His earring, long hair and chewing tobacco went, too.

At the small college he was going to attend we waited in the lobby while he registered. There, playing a pinball machine, was a young man who had on every symbol that people of my generation associate with rebellion and the drug culture. I learned later that he was from Colorado.

By the grace of God I kept from criticizing him to my wife, or even in my mind. Two or three times I was tempted to pray, "Lord, please don't let John get mixed up with the likes of him!" But I didn't.

Three months later the college's student leadership invited me to speak during a chapel service. As part of the program that day the student body had chosen a boy and a girl to give their testimonies because of their outstanding Christian witnesses on campus.

Can you guess who the boy was? The free spirit from Colorado. Sitting on the platform listening to his testimony I was grateful I did not have to repent of false judgment.

Both of these incidents have helped me quit judging others by their outer appearances. Wearing an earring or long hair has little or nothing to do with the inner state of the spirit.

What did I advise Gene to do about *his* son's earring?

"Go home and tell your son what you just told me about your tattoo," I suggested. "And ask his forgiveness for your anger. Forget the earring."

Drawing Lines for the Wrong Reasons

Our experiences with our children gave us lots of opportunities to make mistakes in the area of drawing lines. Fear of what was going on in our world and of how it would affect them, and advice from too many books and seminars on how to raise godly children, caused us to draw too-tight boundary lines for behavior, dress and moral matters. We tried to guard them from evil with fences, forgetting that unless the Lord guards a home, we labor in vain who guard it (to paraphrase Psalm 127:1). I needed to learn that our responsibility is not to raise godly children, but to be godly parents.

Sure, as parents we have the "right" to draw lines wherever we want to: "This is our house and we are paying the bills!" Sound familiar?

Two cautions are in order, here. First, lines drawn too tightly and for superficial reasons like "What will our friends at church think?" often backfire, driving our children away from us, our values and, often, from God.

Remember, our children get their pictures of God from us. Quite frankly, they do not want a God like the frowning, disapproving spoilsport we have often projected! God sees a child's heart and knows that when it is committed to Him, all these peripheral issues will eventually fall into place.

Second, we must be careful not to judge others, especially for behaviors we consider "un-Christian," which, in reality, have little to do with a person's relationship to God. The Bible says, "Do not judge, lest you be judged yourselves. For in the way you judge, you will be judged; and by your standard of measure, it shall be measured to you" (Matthew 7:1–2). Children have an amazing ability to see right through us to all the hypocrisies and inconsistencies in our own lives, such as:

- preaching at them about bad movies while we watch questionable television programs at home;
- preaching about morals while we practice little deceits over the phone and with people who come to our doors;
- acting and talking one way in public and another way in private.

I know you are thinking, *What are Christian parents supposed to do? We have to have rules.*

You are right. We have to have rules, lines drawn to help us train the children God has given us. But we need to make sure we draw them in the right places and over the issues that count.

Understanding Root Causes

It helps to understand the root causes for the kinds of behaviors that are important to young people and bothersome to adults.

Why, for example, did John choose to wear an earring? I do not know for sure, but I would not hesitate to suggest that, since many young men are now wearing earrings, the root cause was peer pressure.

I remember why I started smoking in high school. Smoking was a symbol of manhood, a means of acceptance. In my mind smoking was something I had to do to be accepted by my peers.

It is easy to forget, as we deal with our children and other young people, what we were like and what we did when we were young. Styles and trends may change from generation to generation, but peer pressure remains the same.

We need to remember what the pull of peer pressure felt like. In fact, we need to recognize the pull it has on us now. Such recollections will help us be more sympathetic and understanding with our children, and will help us to draw lines in the right places and over meaningful, not superficial, issues.

Another root cause of what we might consider outrageous behavior or dress may indeed be a child's need to assert his or her independence by choosing to do something forbidden. Dr. Floyd MacCallum, whose psychology lectures influenced hundreds of students at Christian colleges during the '60s and '70s, used to discuss this need, and how he and his wife allowed for it in their children's lives.

Noting that a prime symbol of rebellion during his son's teenage years was hair length and style, and knowing that his son was needing a "cause" over which to "rebel," Dr. MacCallum explained that he gave the boy the privilege of choosing his own hairstyle when he reached the age of thirteen. Now, while Dr. MacCallum didn't *like* the long, somewhat unkempt look so popular at the time, he was wise enough to know that hairstyle had nothing to do with his son's inner state. It was also a fairly harmless mode of rebellion, posing no dangers to the child or to anyone else. So when his son came home with "the look," Dr. MacCallum and his wife gave him just enough static so the boy knew he was not pleasing his parents (and therefore was asserting his independence), but not enough to drive him away or provoke him: "Well, we're not crazy about it, but if that's the way you want to look, I guess you're old enough to make that decision."

What a wise father! He allowed the boy to let off some of the pressure for personal expression that builds up in adolescence, but contained the behavior within bounds he, as a parent, knew were safe and tolerable.

When we ceased to draw lines with John over things like earrings and tobacco we had a much easier time relating to him. We could accept him and not reject him. We could trust God to deal with John in His own time and His own way. This is exactly what has happened.

Where and How to Draw Lines

Yes, we have to draw lines. But God alone can show us where, and even more importantly, how to do so. He can also give us the right attitudes with which to draw them.

Here are some suggestions.

1. Always, always ask God for guidance on where to draw the lines. He knows which issues "count" for which child, and which don't. He cares about your children and will gladly give you His wisdom.

2. Never make rules with the premise "This is what good Christians do." In the first place, if your children are not walking with God they have no reason to act like Christians anyway, so such reasoning will not motivate them. In fact, it will probably turn them off by promoting an inaccurate and unattractive picture of God.

In the second place, in most of the behavioral issues about which we are talking, the premise is simply not true. The Bible offers clear moral guidelines, but on issues of cultural customs, apparel and conformity we need God's specific directions.

3. Avoid accusations about the motives for your children's behavior. My friend Gene made the mistake of accusing his son of piercing his ear out of rebellion. He was judging his son's motives. Judging is wrong; judging *motives* is worse. We can't discern motives without the guidance of the Holy Spirit, and even then we are not to use our knowledge to accuse or condemn, but to intercede for our children before the Father.

4. Never draw a line out of fear. Fear causes us to react, not to respond out of our Christian value system. Draw lines regarding a particular issue only after going to God for guidance and acting in cooperation with Him. If we have received a word of faith for a child, we can trust Him to protect that child from irreparable damage.

5. Never draw a line out of pride. Forget what other people might say about you. Otherwise, you will be guilty of caving in to the same peer pressure you warn your children about. Your child's life and spiritual well-being are much more important than the approval of others.

6. Never draw a line when you are angry. The anger of man does not achieve the righteousness of God (James 1:20). It is possible to draw the right line in the wrong way, and "blow" the whole issue. Go to God *first*, for guidance and an attitude adjustment. Drawing a line for the right reason and in the right spirit can in the long run communicate love, not confrontation.

7. Draw the lines as far apart, as wide as you can. Don't drive your child away over issues that do not matter. The enemy will delight to use our rules, drawn according to our own understanding, not God's (Proverbs 3:5–6), to make our children see Christianity as a set of do's and don't's.

8. Remember that as your children get older you will in all probability need to expand the lines. Again, only the Holy Spirit can give you specific direction in this area.

To conclude, we must operate constantly in faith if we are going to draw fair and clear lines. And faith comes from hearing a word from God. He may use a friend or writer or speaker to give us wisdom, but we need first to be open to hearing from Him about each of our parenting situations. When we have His word, then we can draw lines with the confidence that He will help us uphold them.

16

Letting Them Go— and Letting God Take Over

The process—receiving the word of faith, learning through the walk of faith, cooperating with God in the work of faith, enduring the wait of faith and rejoicing in the fulfillment of faith—may take one year for one child, and thirty years for another. But praise God! "Faithful is He who calls you, and He also will bring it to pass" (1 Thessalonians 5:24). God always makes good on His promissory notes, and when He does, He adds exorbitant interest: blessings beyond our wildest dreams.

"Letting go" is not only a godly pattern for parenting; it also should be a hallmark of the entire process. By letting go I mean relinquishing our children to God and His purposes. Oh, we may say piously, "Our children are only 'on loan' from God." But do we mean it? Or do we clutch them to ourselves like possessions? Are we really willing to relate so intimately to our loving Father God that we can release our children to His work in their lives, and hold tight *only to Him* as we cooperate in the process?

God was willing to let His Child leave the glory of heaven, which was His by rights, to enter our sinful world and accomplish God's work in our lives. And if we think it didn't hurt God to watch Jesus go through all the pains and sorrows of human maturing and then to suffer Calvary, we know little of the depths of His Fatherhood.

But He's God! you say. He is all-powerful and, besides, He knew everything that was going to happen.

This is certainly true. He *is* God, He *is* all-powerful and He *does* know the end from the beginning. But this offers all the more reason why we should entrust Him with our cherished offspring. Just as He let go of His Son for the fulfillment of His perfect purposes, so godly parents must learn to relinquish their children into the loving arms of their heavenly Father.

God spoke to Johnnie along these lines even before Richard left Him. Her experience is so applicable to our needs that I have asked her to share it in her own words.

Johnnie Speaks

There was a big lump in my throat one summer day in 1970 as we waved goodbye to Richard and his friend Joe. They had just been graduated from high school. Now they were headed to California with their surfboards strapped atop Richard's old car. Their destination was Campus Crusade's six-week Intensive Bible Study, but we all knew that was just the ticket to get them to California where things were "happening."

The next morning as I prayed for Richard I felt like an old mother hen wanting to cover him with my wings for protection from all danger. I sat in my room and thought about every bad thing that could possibly happen as he and Joe traveled, and I asked God to protect them from each one.

Then I stretched my imagination further to include protection from all the evils we were hearing about surfers on the beaches in California in those early days of the drug scene. I tucked him under my wings a little tighter as I continued this procedure.

Finally I exhausted my list of bad things from which Richard (and Joe) needed protection. As I strained my mind to be sure there was nothing else, our dear Father said, *Johnnie, if I do all you want Me to do for Richard, I'll never be able to do what I want to do for him.*

What a shock! Didn't God want to be sure my son never had any problems? That's what I wanted.

Yet I knew God well enough to understand in my heart that God loved him even more than I did. Perplexed, I realized I had to decide if I could really entrust my precious son to God's hands if His thinking was so different from mine.

Slowly I began to recount how, time after time, God's loving way had proved to be so much better than anything we could ever have figured for ourselves. When we had stepped out on His Word, He had faithfully gone beyond our limited thoughts on a matter. But could He be trusted to know better than my mother's heart?

I remembered how we had given Richard to the Lord before he was even born. During his years in the home I had felt a keen sense of responsibility to be a good steward for the Lord in caring for our son. Somehow God was letting me know that from now on things were going to be different. I saw that as our children entered new stages of life our "giving them to the Lord" had to be extended to include that stage, too.

After all, I could see the alternatives God was showing me. I could either release my child totally into His all-wise care and His loving hands, or try desperately to figure with my finite mind what was best, and then ask God to do it!

Not without apprehension I hesitantly but deliberately went around Richard's life and clipped each string, releasing him in a brand-new way to our heavenly Father, so He could work as He needed to accomplish His plan. When the transaction was completed, God's wonderful peace began to move into my heart. There had been no room for it as long as my heart was full of fear!

Only God Himself knew how important that encounter with Him would be for me in the days to come. He knew Richard was going to be making some bad decisions in the near future, but He also knew He was free, now, to work them for good in our son's life.

Since then, it has been a deliberate, definite choice to let each of our children go. I could never have done it if I had not seen it as releasing them into God's hands, realizing that the direction of their lives was up to God from that point on. I continue to have to remind myself that my part now is to trust God and them. This requires a new thought pattern regarding our relationships, a pattern that must unfold on a choice-by-choice, situation-by-situation basis.

Praise God for His faithfulness! Four out of five of our children have found God's slots for their lives, and we believe the youngest, now in college, will do the same. Four out of five of our children have found God's special partner for life. Each one is perfect: I could never have chosen as well as our heavenly Father did. And what wonderful grandchildren they have produced!

Truly, we can trust Him to know best for our children.

The process of rearing each of our children may be short and it may be long—but God is faithful. The patterns He gives us to use in the parenting process are reliable and workable. And seeking to conform to His parenting image not only draws us closer to Him, but fits us to serve Him better in other realms of life, as well.

How we need to grasp both the greatness and the practicality of God's Fatherhood! When he "setteth the solitary in families" (Psalm 68:6, KJV), He knew what He was doing.